2021 Christmas

Dearest
Aunt Carol —

Merrey Christmas! ♥
There's nothing like a
positive woman to be around.
I'm lucky + blessed to have one (you)
in my family tree. Blessings

Jodi Dunn

D1016919

A

Lifetime

of Positive

Thinking

Ruth Stafford Peale with President George W. Bush at the White House, April 6, 2001, at meeting of Horatio Alger Awards.

A Lifetime of Positive Thinking

by

RUTH STAFFORD PEALE

with Jo Kadlecek

PEALE CENTER
FOR CHRISTIAN LIVING

The Outreach Division of Guideposts

66 EAST MAIN STREET, PAWLING, N.Y. 12564-1409

ACKNOWLEDGMENTS

All Scripture quotations, unless otherwise noted, are taken from *The King James Version of the Bible.*

Scripture quotations marked (NIV) are taken from *The Holy Bible, New International Version.* Copyright © 1973, 1978, 1984 International Bible Society. Used by permission of Zondervan Bible Publishers.

All photographs within the book are copyright © Peale Center for Christian Living, Pawling, New York.

Jacket designed by Pat Joyce/Peale Center for Christian Living
Interior designed and typeset by José R. Fonfrias
Indexed by Patricia Woodruff
Printed in the United States of America

Dedicated to the memory

of my beloved husband

and

lifelong companion

Dr. Norman Vincent Peale

Contents

Introduction

By Van Varner

I NEVER CALLED Norman Vincent Peale anything but "Dr. Peale." I always call Ruth Stafford Peale, his wife, "Ruth." If I had to do it over again I would still use "Dr. Peale," because as a man of God I respected him, but Ruth, no, I would say "Mrs. Peale." Talk about respect, I have it for her in abundance, for among other accomplishments, Dr. Peale could not have gained his fame, or maybe even written *The Power of Positive Thinking*, without her steadying hand.

Let's go back to 1954. That's when I had my interview for an editorial job at *Guideposts* magazine

---

Van Varner spent more than forty years working with Dr. and Mrs. Peale and *Guideposts* magazine, becoming editor-in-chief in 1981. He has contributed to many publications, including the annual devotional book *Daily Guideposts*.

(founded by Dr. Peale). I had been through Len LeSourd, the editor of *Guideposts,* and Dr. Peale was in his office at 1025 Fifth Avenue for the final meeting. The subject of religion, and I was primed for it, never came up. Instead, after I had displayed my professional wares, he asked me some questions, and the final one was, "Are you a happy man?" I thought about it for a minute, and then, nodding my head, said yes, I had to confess that I was.

Well, I never expected such an outburst. "Ruth," he called to some person in another office, "Come meet a happy Guideposts editor!" That is how I began my forty-four-year history with the magazine and how I met them both in the same day, for in Ruth came, smiling, offering me her hand. I was too excited to pay much attention to her except for the fact that she was married to the big boss. I had yet to learn.

The next time I saw her was a year later at the celebration of Norman and Ruth's twenty-fifth wedding anniversary. The party was held at Marble Collegiate Church. The Peales' children were there: Maggie, twenty-two; John, nineteen; and Liz, thirteen. I got to know Maggie for her writing, and Liz worked for me in a venture at the World's Fair some years later. I saw John only at a distance on special occasions. That day in June 1955, I joined hundreds of people in the receiving line and when I came up to Mrs. Peale, "Van," she said without a moment's hesitation, "how's the happy editor?" With so many people to greet I was amazed that she remembered me, and I mumbled a non-sensible reply. I had yet to learn that, first, she had a politician's knack for remembering names; second, she considered Guideposts an important part of her life; and third, she really meant it when she complimented Van Varner.

Already I was impressed by her, and I was struck, too, by her eyes, blue they were, as blue as Technicolor. What's more, she was slim for a mother of three, and, dressed in a beige garden party dress with a large diaphanous hat, she was beautifully attired. This was a condition that must have been innate, for in all the years since, I have never seen her that she wasn't carefully, appropriately turned out. I can believe the stories I've heard that one reason she liked going to Hong Kong was to shop—but mind you, the dresses there were much cheaper in price than those she could buy in America. I was to discover that she believed in watching every penny, the taking of a dinner bun to eat at breakfast, for instance, or the sharing of a single sandwich with the good Doctor at lunch. Thrift was born in her during the hard years of growing up in Iowa and Michigan, though she never admitted that they were difficult.

She was the daughter of a poor, hardworking Methodist preacher, the Reverend Frank Burton Stafford, and his wife, Anna Loretta. She had two brothers, William, who was older, and Charles, younger. Her memories of the Midwest years are few, or, I think, shelved in the back of her mind as being unimportant. The closeness of family, however, was a lasting birthright. The Staffords were always together. Typical was the Stafford singing group, which performed in church concerts or singing parts at the Clear Lake Iowa Church where the Reverend Stafford was minister. (Ruth was a cute little girl who naturally stole the show.) Ruth was ambitious always and determined early on that she'd go to college. She made it, but after her freshman year at Syracuse University, she dropped out and worked in Detroit for the Michigan Bell Telephone Company to help brother Bill through his senior year.

Think of it! Family was that much of a cardinal tenet with her then, just as it was later. She went back to Syracuse and graduated with the class of 1928. (In 1953 she received an honorary degree of Doctor of Laws.) For two years Ruth taught mathematics in the city of Syracuse's Central High School, all the while insisting that she would never marry a clergyman. So, you see, Ruth could be wrong . . . .

Marriage brought changes. Dr. Peale, despite all that was good about him, was temperamentally volatile, given to moods and an up-and-down personality. Ruth was serious about her marriage vows that made her a helpmate to her husband. Her faith in God was indomitable. She determined that she would develop an even-keeled mien. While he worked on his sermons and speeches, wrote his letters and responded to people, she created an atmosphere that reduced the stress. "Reducing the stress" became Ruth Peale's permanent watchwords.

Dr. Peale came first in her thinking. There would be no distracting noise. She would not raise her voice at any time, either to agree or disagree. In time even their children, when they were fighting as kids do, were silenced with a quiet reprimand. In spite of Dr. Peale's thirty-some years of bachelorhood, he knew little about handling money. (He didn't know how to make a deposit in a savings account and, it is said, he once wrote a check at a bank and it was cashed, though he didn't have an account. It was a Pawling bank and Ruth had the account.) Ruth handled the finances. She checked in and out of hotels and made all travel arrangements. She always drove the car, since she secretly didn't trust him at the wheel. She protected him as a bodyguard and as a blotter for any irritating news, for his natural reaction was to retreat, give up. She had to be a vigilant watchman.

What was the result of all this reduction of stress? She came to the conclusion that she was very capable, an executive-type person, and that delving into the fields that Dr. Peale had no time for, or an inclination for, was something that she was good at, and also, for that matter, that she enjoyed. Ruth realized that she and her husband were an inviolable team, yin and yang, dependent upon one another.

Little wonder that today I have gone to the library and there, in *Who's Who* under her name, are six inches of small type. I don't doubt that her son John, as a little boy, believed that his "mother was busy at the lumber yard" because of all the boards she belonged to. Taking the lead in things that should be done, these things came naturally. At Marble Collegiate Ruth saw to it that Dr. Peale's sermons were preserved and distributed to a waiting public, first by having family and friends working at card tables in the living room (the same tables used in the birth of *Guideposts*), until she actually founded the Foundation for Christian Living. I remember a talk she gave about the sermons. Very affectionately she described how Dr. Peale's words always needed "a bit of tidying." She went on by saying, quite unapologetically, "Behind every great writer stands a great editor." Dr. Peale is credited with never letting a good idea languish; ditto Ruth.

I've felt that Ruth's approach to his and her in-laws should be duplicated by every couple in the world. There was a period when Ruth had "the problem" close at hand, when Loretta Stafford and Charles Peale lived with them. They were opposites in their nature. Charles was a gregarious, fun-loving, cigar-smoking man, and Loretta was sweet in disposition, liked to play the piano, but she was the epitome of the strait-laced minister's wife. As you can imagine, they disliked each other. If you left the room for a second she would fluff up the pillows during the seconds you were gone while Charles would be smoking his cigars and leaving the ashes in, or near, an ashtray; they were, shall I say, different. They may have carried on a private war, but Ruth and Dr. Peale were not affected because of their pact wherein she never said a derogatory word against Charles and Dr. Peale kept quiet about anything negative concerning Loretta.

Year upon year the *Who's Who* listing includes everything, from her positions as the first woman chairman of the National Board of North American Missions in America to the trusteeship of Hope College in Holland, Michigan. The awards are equally staggering, everything from a Distinguished Service Award from the Council of Churches to the first woman to receive a Horatio Alger Award. Who knows which of the many awards was most meaningful, but I suspect that the New York State Mother of the Year came closest, at least in sprit.

In spite of her busy schedule, Ruth was an adoring, responsible parent. She always was at the school's shows or athletics if one of her children was involved. The Christmas pageant was a particular test for her. All three attended New York's Friends Seminary. Liz started at the age of three and loved the pageant. She could not understand the sigh of relief her mother gave after it was over in her senior year, but Liz had not sat through twenty-one years of them! Maggie once called her father "an old goat" over the telephone and he said he'd come home and give her a spanking, which he was about to do, but Ruth quietly talked him out of it. Not that Ruth didn't get angry. The blue of her eyes would suddenly blaze and grow large and the pale centers would take on a lot of fiery activity. That was anger, but she'd stare the disobedient child down, speaking softly to the wrongdoer. Punishment meant extra practice on the piano.

I didn't see much of Ruth in the first days I was at Guideposts. (I have to laugh at the many times we thought the Peales should be tired and ready to quit; it has taken almost half of their lives, and mine, to refute it. They simply do not stop working. Ruth, at ninety-four, is still on the job.) When I took to handling a bit of public relations I saw Ruth often. It started with the World's Fair of '64 and '65. Ruth was on the board of the Protestant Center, and she asked my partner Harold Hansen and me to develop an exhibit for Guideposts at the Center's building. We jumped at the chance and came up with an acceptable plan. (Liz Peale, grown up, was one of the people we hired as a receptionist.)

During this time I got to know another side of Ruth; she was always there when the cards were down; she was always a trooper. When it was the magazine's Youth Writing Contest, she and the Doctor were in Washington for the award to a teenager, for the Writer's Workshop, she and the Doctor always drove over to Rye and started the week off with dinner and an informal speech; the annual Church Award was another obligation for the Peales, but on one occasion in Houston the Doctor couldn't come and Ruth went into the breech. She gave a fine talk. But the one award I most certainly applaud Ruth for was in Macon, Georgia. It was a church with about thirty members, all of them were mentally retarded, yet they

played the piano, gave a kind of sermon, and conducted a service that brought tears to my eyes. The only
people invited to attend were the Peales and the gov-
ernor, Jimmy Carter, and Rosalyn. Dr. Peale was suddenly ill and I was forced to take his place. Ruth, that
day, made me feel like Norman Vincent Peale, and it
was a treat.

The Peales have been everywhere, done everything,
and have been close to people of power. They have
been houseguests of Chiang Kai-shek and overnight
visitors in the White House, but those were the special
occasions—the un-special were just as meaningful.
(They even came for an intimate dinner at my apartment, just the three of us.). They are a little awed by
grandeur and elegance, but each remained the simple
Midwesterner at heart, and Ruth, especially, is
untouched by flattery. I watched a man (I won't say
who) eager to impress her pour on the compliments.
She simply looked mystified and moved on.

I mentioned at the start of this piece the respect I have
for Ruth. That respect has grown over the years and never
so profoundly as it has since Dr. Peale's death on
Christmas Eve, 1993. For any two people as closely
entwined as they were, I dreaded what the separation
would bring. Ruth and most of the family were with him
when he died. As he struggled to hold on to life, Ruth

leaned close to him and said very softly, "It's all right, you can let go now." And gradually, he let go. For Ruth it was the beginning of a new life for Dr. Peale. "Because I live," Jesus said, "ye shall live also" ((John 14:19).

Why should I have worried about how she would take the loss? Faith was her security, and there was work to be done. To this day she has not stopped. Ruth continues to lead the Guideposts board meetings with her customary snap. She has favored the revolutionary introduction of advertising in Guideposts publications (provided it is tastefully done) just as surely as she was the one person in the organization who alerted them to the computer age. She has been active in merging the Foundation for Christian Living with Guideposts and renaming it the Peale Center for Christian Living; she has traveled (carrying her own suitcase), made speeches (some people say they are better than ever, I for one). She spoke to a jammed service of the Crystal Cathedral in 1996 that was televised to millions on *The Hour of Power* program. It was remarkable. All this, and more, and she is well into her tenth decade. Ruth warns that she expects a celebration at the Waldorf-Astoria on Park Avenue when she gets to be a hundred. They had better get ready.

Proof that she was serious came when Ruth slipped and fell one day in 1998. She broke her hip. So, she had a period of repair in a nearby home for senior citizens. And what did that mean? Nothing, except a minor inconvenience. She worked just the same as though she hadn't had the fall. She forced herself, got into therapy, and in no time was taking her daily walk back at home.

Ruth has admitted to a pang of loneliness in the beginning without her husband of sixty-three years. She goes on living alone in the big house known as the Hill Farm (her two daughters have homes nearby). She would come back after a busy day at the office and the empty house would hit her like a cold draft of air. She would think about how worried Dr. Peale would be if she were half an hour overdue in returning home. There was that kind of dependence. She would turn on the radio—there was always a certain comfort in hearing a human voice. And. she would grab hold of herself, take her walk about the farm, enjoying the beauty of the hills. If a wisp of sadness strayed in, she'd just sit at her desk, fold her hands, and love Him.

One Sunday evening Ruth was sitting alone in the family room at Hill Farm when the telephone rang.

"Grandma," exclaimed her granddaughter Becca from New York City, "are you all right?"

"Of course, Becca. Why do you ask?"

"I had a dream. Grandpa came to me and said clearly,

'Tell Grandma to turn on the alarm. Do it now, Becca.' And then I woke up and just had to call you."

When they were finished with the conversation, Ruth got up and turned on the security system. Then she wondered, "Did Norman somehow look down from heaven and put a thought in Becca's head to call?" For Ruth it only meant one thing: The Lord used this experience to remind her that Norman was very much alive and with Him, and that their love will always be with her.

1

*My View
from the
Hill*

The foundation of God standeth sure....

—II Timothy 2:19

*N*OT LONG AGO, I had a moment to sit and relax on the porch of the big white farm house on Quaker Hill, in Pawling, New York, that my husband Norman and I bought many years ago. Even though I am ninety-four years old, I'm usually running from appointment to appointment at the Peale Center or spending time with my grandchildren. But on this day I decided to take a little time just to sit and look across the valley, to feel the fresh country air on my face and take in the full colors of the scene before me. As I did, I was thankful for the many memories that popped into my head while I looked across the open space. Perhaps it was the green of the trees or the white of the clouds that reminded me of wonderful December nights, but for some reason, Christmas Eve memories held me captive for a few minutes on the porch that day.

When our children were young, Norman and I would gather them around the tree and help them put delicate ornaments on each branch. We'd sing Christmas carols together and Norman would read to us from the

Christmas story in the second chapter of Luke. We'd listen each year as if it were the first time we had heard it. The children would sit around their father, hanging on every word, engrossed in the wonderful story of how God sent the baby Jesus to earth to show us His enormous love.

When Norman finished, each child would ask if he or she could open one gift, to which, of course, I would say, "No, children, you have to wait till the morning." The moaning only lasted a moment, though, as the wonder of such anticipation, grounded in the joy of our family tradition, captured their attention again. Then we'd tuck them into bed, kiss them good night and go downstairs to take care of last minute gifts or duties. Christmas was always a joyous time when age-old beliefs intersected with excitement about the future.

I smiled on the porch as I remembered those Christmas Eves, and then it occurred to me how much they can teach us now. As we enter a new year, a new decade, indeed a new century and millennium, I believe it is time to revisit some important lessons of our past in order to prepare for our future. Norman often said that in order to keep growing you've got to keep going back to the gifts and values and attitudes God has given you. If you don't, you get distracted and lose your way. I'm afraid we live in a time when it seems as if many people

have lost their way. That's why it is time to remember—
in order to grow.

You know, I never fully imagined what approaching a
new century might be like. I never imagined what it
would be like to look back over one that has been so full
of change and tragedies and incredible events. As the
"other half" of the man who wrote the now-classic *The
Power of Positive Thinking*, I've learned a few things
these past ninety-plus years that have helped me along
the way, and I'd like to share them with you here. I hope
my experiences will help you too.

On the porch of the farm house that day, I also recalled
many other things. For instance, I saw in the distance a
cluster of houses, and as I thought of the families who
lived there, I remembered the many vacations our family
took, the many moments we shared to create a positive
sense of home. Across the way, I noticed the church
steeple and thanked God for the way He had been the
center of our lives. I saw His earth, the trees and the
fields, and I thought of the blessing of work He'd given
so many of us. I thought of the friends who encouraged
us to keep going, the faith and prayers we had held onto
in the midst of the difficult times. Everything I saw
reminded me of the gifts of the great and full life I've
been able to live in this century. All of these things
reminded me of their importance for the future.

No, we mustn't forget some basic priorities that can anchor us in the days ahead. Norman used to tell people, "Think big, pray big, believe big, act big." If ever there was a time when we needed "big" thinking and praying, it's now. In our view of God, church, marriage, families, work, adversities and other areas of our life, we need to think big again, to hold on to the time-tested principles that have made people survive and flourish throughout the centuries. That is what this book is about.

2

Starting with God

Be still, and know that I am God....

—PSALM 46:10

RECENTLY, a middle-aged woman walked up to me and asked me if I thought a person could still be a positive thinker, even if she didn't believe in God. She looked me square in the eye and asked with utmost sincerity, "If you just want to be a better person and you see positive thinking as a way to be a better person who can do bigger and better things, but you leave God out of it, does it still work for you?"

I looked into this woman's face for a few seconds and wondered about her question. For a moment, I felt sad for her. But I had to be honest with her, so I told her that I had never tried it. Then I continued, "I think there's a danger in thinking that you can leave God out of your life and still be successful, at least as I define success." She was curious. I told her that I didn't deny that, for instance, there were people who had attained financial success by using positive thinking that was separate from Christian living. I was sure they probably had not experienced the same depth of success that they would experience if they believed in God. She frowned and told me she would think about God some more. Then she walked away.

And so that is where we will begin this book. With God. Because I believe long-term satisfaction and success always starts with God. Money can buy you many things, but it cannot buy you such things as love, trust, joy and peace. I know some people might argue with me on this point, but I believe they are missing something I've experienced in the almost ninety-five years I've been alive, something that has made all the difference.

You see, I believe in God. And I am not afraid to tell you that. I grew up in a home where we turned to God regularly. We read the Bible together every day, and my mother and father offered a prayer as part of our daily routine. Then I married a man who turned to God regularly, even daily. Norman had a wonderful habit of telling people that no matter what troubles or challenges they encountered—and challenges would surely come—they could overcome them with the help of God. We raised our three children to turn to God each day, encouraging them develop a personal relationship with God in their everyday life.

"Call on God for answers to your everyday problems," I'd tell them over and over, "and it's amazing how often your solutions will come." And now I say the same thing to my grandchildren. I feel that it's really because of God that I've been able to accomplish things throughout my life, such as becoming publisher and Chairman of the

Board of Guideposts, which Norman and I founded. I've enjoyed working as a member of the board of directors for such ministries and organizations as the American Bible Society, the Interchurch Center, Institutes of Religion and Health, and the Laymen's National Bible Committee—all fine ministries that help people remember God as the starting point of each day they live, the answer to every problem they encounter.

With each passing year, my belief has changed only in that, as Norman used to say, I've sensed God's presence more and more in the every day. Just a few years ago I fell one morning and broke my hip. My daughter Elizabeth, who lives with her family down the road from me with her family, quickly got me medical help. Since the doctors told me how important rest would be for my recovery, I had to cancel some speaking appointments and meetings. It wasn't an easy time for me and sometimes I wanted to give up; still, I knew God was with me and by turning to Him for strength, I got through the long rehabilitation process. He also reminded me of all the wonderful things I had to be thankful for. Even now I'm growing more confident of His presence—and my hip is fine. I even walk two miles every day! To be honest, I do not know how people make it these days without a personal relationship with God through Jesus Christ.

The other day, in fact, I received a very thoughtful letter from a man who said he didn't believe in God even though he was raised to do so. He wrote, "Would you tell me why I should believe in God?" It was a good letter from an obviously fine and thoughtful person, but it also was a challenge. In my reply, I invited him to consider the beauty of nature. I was writing him at the time of year when the leaves were turning glorious colors, and in the New York countryside it was beautiful everywhere you looked. I reminded him that wherever he went, to the mountains, for instance, and saw the tops of the mountains covered with snow, he had to admit the beauty was almost unbelievable.

"You can't think of all the forces of nature," I wrote, "without realizing that there was a mind behind it, a creative Designer who knew what He was doing. And that mind was God's." I ended my letter by encouraging him to remember how fortunate we are if we learn that truth in our youth so we can also learn how God can direct our lives as adults.

You could say I was one of the fortunate ones who learned early on the importance of a God-centered life. Born in Fonda, Iowa, on my parents' fifth wedding anniversary, I was their "wooden-anniversary present," as Dad liked to say. I was the second child in the family and the only girl. My brother Chuck was three years older, and two years after I was born, my brother Bill came along. Our family was then complete.

The small towns of my early childhood and the parsonages where my father ministered are a blur in my mind (I was born, after all, in 1906!). It wasn't until we moved to Detroit when I was seven or eight, and settled into a modest house on Clairmont Avenue, that things began to have a degree of permanence for me.

As I look back today, my childhood seems like a happy, well-ordered dream. I loved playing jacks on the sidewalks or porch steps, and I was a fanatical ropeskipper. I walked to and from school, almost a mile each way, and never once considered it a hardship. It was just something we did.

All through my formative years, the sense of family solidarity and security was strong. We children didn't have many material possessions, but we had peace of mind and the room to grow that came from a balanced combination of love and discipline inside the home. We had a lot of fun with music. Some of Mother's talent was passed along to all of us, and we spent a lot of time around the piano, harmonizing favorite songs and hymns.

God was an important part of our life, but I don't remember being self-conscious about that or feeling that ours was an ultra-pious religion. Our faith in God was simply something we lived. We said grace at meals. We observed quiet days on Sunday after worship services— no movies, no noisy games. From the start, my own faith in the Creator seemed as natural as breathing. Unlike some friends today who I know have struggled simply to believe, I never seemed to have any intellectual doubts to resolve or any great internal conflicts about God's existence. I simply believed the Christian story and message, and drew strength when I needed it from my prayers and my faith. Throughout high school, work, college, marriage, motherhood (now grandmotherhood!), and a very active ministry, God has been my greatest source of help.

Although I never expected to be a pastor's wife, marrying Norman Vincent Peale certainly helped deepen my faith and awareness of God. Norman lived his religion truer than anyone I've ever known. In fact, I've never known anyone who loved life in all its aspects more than he did. Sometimes he wore me out! But he would say that he tried to keep as close as possible to the Source of all energy, and to live in such a way that the channels through which that energy came were always open. In other words, he'd tell me, anyone can live that way and receive that energy from God.

For over fifty years of marriage, Norman and I kept God at the center of our relationship. We believed that

Christianity is not just a musty set of ancient beliefs, or a collection of rules. It is a personal relationship with Jesus Christ, which provides a storehouse of endless joy and energy, and the key that unlocks the storehouse is faith in God. It is a critical component for anyone who wants to have a positive influence on others and live a successful life.

But I also know that that is not always easy, nor is it always popular in these times, times many leaders are calling the "post-modern" (or post-Christian) era. For instance, once I was at a meeting with a group of church denominational officials. Discussion and debate had gone on for hours about certain doctrinal matters. If I recall correctly, the discussion centered around the question of whether or not, in this particular denomination, women should be ordained. Finally, one young minister said something that got everyone's attention.

"Wouldn't it be nice," he said as a smile crossed his face, "if we could just live our religion without arguing about it?!"

It certainly would. And it's not only church officials who are guilty of this. There are too many families in which religion begins with formal churchgoing, hymn singing, Bible reading or other religious activities, but sadly, that's where it ends.

Don't misunderstand me. I know that religious activities are important and necessary ingredients in a life of faith. But I also think that believing in God should simply be lived as a part of our everyday life. That belief should come to the rescue of people who need help. It should soften all judgments with tolerance and compassion. It should help all members of a family over the hurdles and roadblocks they encounter.

Once, when my youngest daughter Elizabeth was seven or eight, she came home from school in tears. Some young friend had been mean to her—or so she said. She was through with Becky, she sobbed. She would never speak to her or play with her again. The more she went on, the angrier and more resentful she became.

Finally, I asked her, "What do you know about Becky's home life?"

She looked up at me as if she'd just been caught in the cookie jar and admitted she knew little or nothing about Becky.

"I happen to know that it's not a very happy one," I told my daughter. "Becky's parents are divorced. Her mother has married again, and Becky doesn't get along with her stepfather. Her real father, whom she loves, never comes to see her. She's an unhappy, confused little girl. Maybe she did act badly toward you, but I don't think it's because she dislikes you. It's because there's great unhappiness and loneliness in her life. So try to be understanding, will you?"

Elizabeth nodded her head and said perceptively, "You mean, she's taking it out on me?"

This was just a simple little family scene, but I think it shows religion in action in daily life. *Judge not,* says the Bible. That was a lesson, and I think my young daughter learned it. In fact, I know she did, because I've since seen Elizabeth's compassion and understanding toward others develop in a remarkable way throughout her adult life!

Believing in God is really love in action. It's caring—really caring—about what another person feels, or says, or is. You don't even have to know the person. For instance, one Christmas, a married couple we know took their small children to a store, gave them each some money, and told them to pick out something for a less privileged child their own age. They were to select it with care because it might be the only present that child received. The children were interested at once. With great concentration, they went about the business of picking out a special gift for another child they didn't know. No one had quoted the golden rule to them, but they were following it, and they discovered the joy of giving.

This example has always encouraged me because it seems that there's a greater influence today pertaining to everyday life and religion than when I was growing up in the 1920s. Consider how much more Christian information has been made available to people in the past few decades alone than when I was a child. I really only remember thinking of the Bible as a source of help and direction for people. Now, with all the Christian books, videos, magazines and tapes available, I believe we've been given a wonderful opportunity to bring religion away from the sort of "super spiritual, way out there" feeling and into our daily lives, where people can learn to talk to God in everyday conversations. People feel they can turn to God for answers to their problems. I know Norman always emphasized that. So did my father, who was also a minister; he liked to emphasize stories from the Bible and use examples from the disciples applicable in everyday life. He was practical in a different way.

I think people's attitudes about God have changed because of all the incredible work that has been done for God in the past fifty years. When I was growing up, many people in our country viewed God as a distant, revered, almost impersonal entity. Now, people feel closer to a spiritual power, and find themselves asking God for help. When people today decide to change careers, for instance, they want help knowing if they're making the right decision. So often they'll go to a quiet place where they can listen to God. Even though the world is a more complex place, people are turning to a spiritual life much more than I can remember in my early life. We think of the world today as smaller than when I was growing up, probably because of technology, and people often feel more connected. But when I was young, the world seemed big and church was about the only way to bring people together.

But one thing hasn't changed in all these years: our need to start each day with God. People still ask me sometimes if I really believe that there is a supernatural force or power that intervenes in human affairs, sometimes providing answers to problems, sometimes exerting a subtle influence on thought processes, sometimes arranging or rearranging the complex pattern of human existence so that desirable goals can be reached. And I always tell them, yes, I firmly believe that there is such a force and that the correct name for it is God. I believe that He does indeed take part in human affairs. I believe that we can ask Him to do so. And this whole process is something called guidance.

Norman and I both believed implicitly in the availability of divine guidance. We asked for it all the time, and I still do. For years, we asked that all three of our children would be guided to marriage partners with whom they could build strong, happy, and successful homes. Today when I look at our family photographs, I know that God heard those prayers. We couldn't have found better spouses for our children ourselves! In turn, they've become committed parents, raising their own really talented and wonderful children (I'm not biased!). So this habit of calling on God has been one that has continued through many, many years, and taken form in many, many ways.

I remember often going to Norman's office whenever he needed to talk through a sermon or speech. Norman often just talked to the Lord as if He were right there listening (which we know He is). "Lord," he'd say, "we have this problem. You know what it is without our telling. Please guide us in the right direction. Make us receptive to Your will. We thank You for this help that You are now giving us."

Then we'd sit quietly for a while. We never concentrated on the specific problem or on possible solutions. Instead, we tried to make our minds quiet and receptive. Sometimes, I'd think of some appropriate phrase from the Bible and focus on that. "Be still, and know that I am God," Psalm 46:10 says. Or, "In quietness and confidence shall be your strength," wrote the prophet Isaiah (30:15). After a while, one of us would say to the other, "It seems to me this is the way to deal with this." Or, "I believe we've been on the wrong track with this one. Perhaps we should handle it this way." It was uncanny how often the same conviction came to both of us, and how often a clear line of action would open up where things were obscure before.

But how can you be sure you're on the receiving end of guidance? One pretty good indication, I think, is when the answer that comes is not necessarily the one you'd prefer. The best example of this in our lives was the time a few years after we were married in 1930. We were living in Syracuse, New York, where Norman was pastor of the University Methodist Church. We were both happy there and enjoyed many friends. Then, suddenly, Norman received calls from two very important churches. One was in Los Angeles—the largest Methodist congregation in the country. The other came from a beautiful church in New York City called Marble Collegiate Church.

One of Norman's basic characteristics was indecision —during his entire life he had a tendency to vacillate, a reluctance to make up his mind. I think the chief reason was that he had a great gift for seeing all sides of a question, which is a tremendous asset when counseling a quarreling couple. But that same gift could be a distinct problem in his own personal life when all sides of a question seemed to cancel each other out, leaving Norman paralyzed, unable to move in any direction.

This is exactly what happened when those simultaneous calls came from two good churches. Of course, a third possibility was to refuse both calls and stay where we were. But there was little doubt that a greater ministry was awaiting us on either the East Coast or the West. The question was which one to accept.

At first, Norman did the natural thing and asked the advice and counsel of his family, friends and associates in Syracuse. Everyone had firm opinions and very good reasons to back up those opinions. Norman would listen to one set of arguments and begin to lean in one direction. Then a conflicting set would be presented and he would lean the other way. He made up his mind and then changed it several times. It was a nerve-racking strain not only on him, but on everyone around him. Meanwhile, time was running out. Both churches needed an answer.

Finally, one day after lunch, I suggested we go into our living room. After closing the door, I looked at my husband and said, "Norman, this can't go on. We're not going to leave this room until you've come to a decision. And to come to that decision we're going to do what we should have done in the first place. We're going to put it in God's hands. We're going to ask for His guidance and wait for it and listen for it until we get it, no matter how long it takes."

We stayed in that room all through the afternoon and far into the evening. We knelt at times by an old chintz-covered couch and held hands and prayed. There were long periods of silence. Norman would pace, and I would sit. We both would turn the pages of the Bible. But no answer came.

I had been quite sure Norman's preference was to go to California. Many things about it appealed to him: the climate, his best-loved college friends who lived there, the simplicity and openness of Californians. Besides, he was pleased and flattered by the thought of preaching to what was then the largest Methodist congregation in the country, if not the world. He felt sure he would be happy in California.

As for New York, he seriously doubted his ability to reach or help a sophisticated Fifth Avenue congregation. He was afraid that his popular approach would be frowned upon by people who expected profound theology. He had heard that the great nave of the Marble Church, capable of seating at least twelve hundred people, seldom had a third that many. Furthermore, he had been told that Fifth Avenue at 29th Street was a bad location—too far downtown (which is funny to think about in the year 2000!). It was said that industry was moving into that area and residents were moving out. That seemed to mean that the church had nowhere to go but down. Finally, the Marble Church was a different denomination—Reformed Church in America. Norman felt that there were not many great theological differences, but he had always been a Methodist. His father was a Methodist minister, and there were strong ties of tradition and sentiment for us both to the Methodist Church.

All of this was in my mind as we prayed and waited. I knew it was in Norman's mind too. But we tried as hard as we could to surrender any shred of personal preference and leave the whole thing up to the Lord. We must have said, "Thy will be done," a hundred times.

Suddenly the atmosphere in the room seemed to change. Instead of the uncertainty and urgent seeking, we felt a relaxation of tension. It was almost as if some great silent clock had struck a deep, decisive note. Norman looked at me and said simply, "Do you have an answer?"

"Yes," I answered, "I do, but you must make this decision. Have you an answer?"

Suddenly, Norman was firm. "I have indeed. I believe God wants us to go to New York." The same guidance had come to me.

A few hours before, Norman would instantly have cited to me all the good reasons for going to California. But now he seemed sure that New York was where God wanted us. "In that case," I suggested, "why don't you pick up the telephone right now and call New York to tell them you're coming?"

Silently, Norman walked over to the telephone and put in the long-distance call. Later he told me that all feelings of doubt were gone at that moment. He announced to the New York official that he would be honored to accept the call to Marble Collegiate Church. Then he sent a telegram to Los Angeles expressing his regret that he could not accept their call. After all the days of anguished indecision, he exuded a calmness and a resoluteness about his decision that was simply amazing. He showed no sense of frustration or personal disappointment, just an acceptance of being led—being guided by God in the right direction.

Was it the right direction? Well, all I can say is that the powerful West Coast church had to struggle with a downtown location, and finally its great edifice was used for other purposes. In the beginning, things were not easy at Marble Church either—the dead hand of the Depression lay heavy still on the city. People were out of work and short on hope. But gradually the Power that guided us there saw to it that the empty pews were filled to overflowing, not just for one service every Sunday morning, but for two services! Years later, worshipers in overflow auditoriums even watched over closed-circuit television.

Why did God want Norman and me to go to New York? I can't pretend to know the mind of God, but it seems at least possible that God knew how Norman's message of hope, encouragement and spiritual buoyancy was needed more urgently in New York, where the mood of the people was approaching despair at that dark time in our country's economic history. I think God also orchestrated it so that on weekends in the great impersonal city, thousands of lonely souls who had nothing to do and nowhere to go, young people who needed a place to make friendships, old people who missed the warm religious ties that they had known in smaller communities, all could feel welcomed at Marble Collegiate Church. We never gave any thought to such considerations when we tried to solve the dilemma with our fallible human minds. But God knew about them all the time.

In the full and crowded years that have passed since that night in Syracuse, I have felt this guidance from God work in my life countless times. Often it happens right in church on Sunday morning. Time and again, sitting in the pew, I heard Norman depart from the outline of his sermon to make a point that had just occurred to him spontaneously, and then after the service someone would mention to me how moved she or he had been by Norman's message. I have sensed God's direction at

Guideposts or in board meetings when I knew the organization I was serving needed a little push. I know that in raising our children, and watching them raise theirs, God's guidance has been a cornerstone and constant strength. And as I've traveled all over the world, sitting with world leaders, presidents, and important men and women of business, as I've visited colleges, universities, conferences and churches, I've continually recognized the importance of a personal belief in God. It is critical for anyone who wants to live a good and successful life in the next century. I believe it is as critical as the colors are in a sunset, such as the one I watched from our Quaker Hill porch last week. That sunset was brilliant beyond description. Overhead, white clouds floated through the blue sky. As the sun reached the horizon, its red glow spread for miles in both directions. I sat enthralled. Only God could produce such beauty.

Some people radiate an indescribable glow, as beautiful as any sunset, that changes the atmosphere whenever they enter a room. They have a loving spirit that brings joy and disperses tension. I know several people who have this gift, and I'm sure you do, too. What is the secret? Simply, it's having an awareness of God's presence in their own lives that lights up everything around them. They believe in God, and ask Him daily to "make his face to shine upon" them (Numbers 6:25).

They know that starting with God is the secret to positive living!

> ~~✳~~ TAKE IT WITH YOU ✳~~
>
> *"Call on God for answers to your everyday problems, and it's amazing how often your solutions will come!*
> *And don't forget to live your faith!"*

3

When Church Is the Cornerstone

For where two or three are gathered together in my name, there am I in the midst of them.

—MATTHEW 18:20

FOR AS LONG as I can remember I have gone to church on Sunday mornings. As a little girl, I enjoyed sitting in the small Methodist church in Iowa (and later in Michigan) where my father was the pastor, hearing his gentle voice recount the stories of the Bible to the congregation. I'd listen to him say the Lord's Prayer as I sat between my brother and my mother. Every now and then, I'd wiggle in the pew as children often do, until my mother's soft hand would tap my knee and my father's tender glance would come my way from his big pulpit. I loved sitting with my family, looking up at the stained glass windows and hearing the other families sing hymns before my minister-father would give us his sermon each week. Church was the cornerstone of our family and our faith. And it was the center of almost every Christian community across the country in those days, the glue that held people together when times got hard.

But I never expected to become a minister's wife. It was actually the last thing I wanted to be. By my junior year of college at Syracuse University, in 1927, I had moved into a sorority house with four roommates. One of them, Phyllis Leonard, was the daughter of a bishop, and we used to talk for hours about the pros and cons of having a minister as a father. We proclaimed—and our roommates loudly agreed—that the last thing we'd ever do was marry a minister, with all the self-denial and self-discipline and lack of privacy that such a role required. We all knew from first-hand experience that it was not easy living up to those kind of expectations!

Of course, God was in charge of our lives, and per-haps our marriages were a manifestation of His sense of humor. I suppose we didn't fully appreciate then that church was exactly the right place to meet friends, and even a future husband!

Many of the girls at my sorority house who went to Norman's church on Sundays came back sighing romanti-cally about the handsome young minister—miraculously unmarried at the age of twenty-nine—who held his con-gregation spellbound with sermons so eloquent and enthusiastic that going to church became an adventure, not an obligation (which of course is how it's supposed to be). This young Methodist minister emphasized that Christian faith could be a joyous, exciting, life-giving experience—every day, not just on Sundays. He had a great sense of humor that appealed particularly to young people; sometimes waves of laughter swept over the congregation of the stately University Methodist Church. Outside the church he was said to be friendly, sociable and easygoing. Yet when he stood in the pulpit, everyone respected his great spiritual authority.

"You really ought to meet him, Ruth," Phyllis told me. "Or at least come to hear him preach. He's from the Midwest, like you—Ohio, I think. I know you'd like him."

I groaned. "That just the trouble," I replied. "The last thing I want to do is find myself liking an unmarried minister."

To this day, I wonder sometimes if the spiritual side of our nature—which is timeless—has the gift of knowing what might lie ahead. As Emerson said, "The soul contains the event that shall befall it." It may be fanciful, but I believe that something in me even then was dimly aware that my destiny was linked with this popular young man all the girls were talking about. My conscious mind, determined to avoid any relationships with ministers, rejected these signals so strongly I kept thinking up excuses not to even hear him preach. I was too busy. I had too many dates. I was going to another church. Yes, I had plenty of good excuses.

And then one night Phyllis persuaded me to go with her to a party being given by the young people's group at the church. And just to stop her from harping on the subject any longer, I decided to join her.

It was an exciting evening and I chatted with many interesting young people. By the time Phyllis and I were about to leave, she turned to me and whispered, "Ruth, you haven't even met Norman Peale. Come on, I'll introduce you!"

Before I could argue, she steered me across the room and said, "Mr. Peale, this is my roommate, Ruth Stafford."

We shook hands. And then a surprising thing happened. He held my hand just a fraction of a second longer than was necessary! I thought to myself, "This is going to be interesting!"

And of course it has been ever since. Dating Norman for the next three years meant I spent a lot of time in church. For obvious reasons, it didn't let up when we married, either—after all, he did have to be in church every Sunday to preach! Then while Norman was counseling or teaching in the church, I was able to serve on countless committees and ministry boards for our church and the denomination. We also had the great joy of raising our three children with a deep respect and appreciation for church. They, too, have raised their children with the same recognition that regular worship services and fellowship with other Christians is a staple for positive, fruitful living. And now, in my nineties, I have found church is still a critical part of my life.

When Norman and I first went to Marble Collegiate Church, we struggled initially. In fact, our first six years there occurred at a time when there was little growth and little change in the country. People were economically depressed. It was hard for many to put food on the table to feed their families, and it was hard to help them see beyond their circumstances. But they never stopped believing in God, and many of them found that the more they came to church, the better their lives—or at least their attitudes—became.

Things are quite different these days. Today, I feel we're struggling to find our way through a time of spiritual depression in our country. That's why I'm convinced that people in this new century will need to feel a responsibility to restore the values on which their faith is based. We have detoured to the point that we can't put a nativity scene in a city square or say a prayer in a public school, which I think is quite sad. Recently, in one city, someone even objected because a little boy at an elementary school was in an attitude of prayer during the lunch period. Maybe we have come to this difficult juncture because church no longer is at the center of peoples' lives. Some people have told me that they can believe in God on their own, and don't need organized religion. Others tell me their friends call them "weird" if they attend church on a regular basis. Who needs all that guilt and all those rules, they are asked. Well, I am not sure a rigid church is the kind of church I'd like to go to either, but that doesn't mean we should not go at all.

Church might not be the central institution in our society the way it was when I was younger, yet many churches today still do have practical programs to help people with their every day lives. I know of several churches, for instance, that offer regular marriage retreats or counseling for couples who might be struggling. Others present a variety of activities for young people, whether it is involvement in Sunday school, service projects or social events. There are beautiful services that allow musicians and artists to share their gifts with the rest of the congregation, and creative ways to get outsiders involved, such as sports leagues or organized tours to foreign countries.

As I travel and speak to different organizations at banquets, I try to encourage people to find a church where they can be comfortable, where they will be surrounded by persons of like desire for their spiritual life, and where they are serving in a community. Then they should become active in that church in some way, whether volunteering for outreach ministries or ushering during services or hosting a small group. The point is you must give if you're going to get, and if you believe in God you must try to develop good relationships with other believers. I also tell people that as a result of this kind of approach to church, all of my children and grandchildren are finding ways to make a difference in their church communities.

What I'm trying to say is that church has never gone out of style nor lost its importance in our lives. Of course, sometimes it can get, well, a little sticky at times. I'll always remember the time a little boy was visiting New York City for the first time and his parents brought him to a Sunday service at Marble Collegiate. The family sat in the balcony where they had a fine view of everything. Norman was in rare form that morning, and his sermon was full of stories taken from everyday life, many of which had their humorous side. The little boy looked down in wonder at all the laughing faces, the turned to his parents.

"This can't be church," he whispered seriously, "everybody's having fun!" You can imagine the confused but excited looks on their faces when we greeted them after the service.

And I can never forget those times one winter when I took our children on sightseeing or investigating tours— the kind of thing you always put off doing. We went to the New York City bus terminal, at the time the largest in the world, with the fastest escalator. We went out to see the Statue of Liberty and up the Empire State Building. There were lots of out-of-the-way places we explored. We had a wonderful time.

As you know, sometimes youngsters can get a bit carried away by the spirit of fun. One summer afternoon when Margaret was about ten and John was about eight, we had postponed our exploring plans. On this particular day, I was having a very serious meeting of church women in our apartment. Suddenly the doorbell buzzed, and there was one of the doormen of the building, looking grave. "Mrs. Peale," he said, "there's a policeman downstairs. He has a complaint. Apparently, someone is dropping bombs from your apartment windows and onto the street."

"Bombs?!" I echoed incredulously.

"Water bombs," clarified the doorman. "Paper bags filled with water to make them fall on people's heads. There's a policeman with an angry lady whose clothes are all splashed."

"People's heads?" In the sudden hush behind me, I could sense all the visiting churchwomen listening intently.

"You mean our children are dropping these, these things on passersby? How do you know *our* children are the culprits?" Behind me I could almost feel the craning of necks and the raised eyebrows. It was one of those rare moments when I wished I hadn't been involved in a church!

"Because, Mrs. Peale," the doorman whispered, "your children have been practicing their—er—bombing techniques in the air shaft inside the building. The bottom of the shaft is full of water and sand and paper bags. I'm afraid Margaret and John are the guilty ones. No doubt about it."

I summoned the guilty ones and sent them in disgrace to their rooms. Then I had to go downstairs, placate the policeman, apologize to the irate lady, arrange to pay for having her clothes cleaned, assure the doorman that such an aerial assault would never happen again, and then I had to—gulp—face the women from my church.

Thankfully, they all murmured something about "kids being kids" as they left, graciously telling me they had had a fruitful meeting. Norman and I spoke sternly that night to our children, explaining that someone could have been hurt. We made them clean up the debris. They also were to pay from their allowance for the lady's cleaning bill. After all was said and done, I must confess that Norman and I were a bit relieved and grateful that our children did have a sense of fun—even if it was a bit misguided at the time. We were glad that they weren't meek and mild goody-goodies, that they were

high-spirited and fun-loving even if they were preacher's kids.

So church life often comes with challenges and quirks
because that's how we humans are—full of challenges
and quirks. And that's what makes up each little congregation in each corner of our country. It is also the
place where God has said He would dwell—as Scripture
says, whenever two or three are gathered in His name,
there He is in their midst. Perhaps that is also why
church can also be one of the best places to counter the
deep sense of loneliness we all feel at some time or
another.

I get many letters at the Peale Center for Christian
Living from people who tell me story after story of
aching loneliness. "I'm so tired of being lonely and going
places by myself," many have written. It is a problem
that affects each of us at some time. None of us can get
through life without feeling some loneliness. I read a
report several years ago from a UCLA social psychologist stating that ten percent of the American population
feels lonely at any given time. I'm sure the number today
is much higher as technology can often take us further
away from live human contact. And considering most
people are afraid to admit they feel lonely these days, it
would be difficult to gauge just how much of our population suffers from loneliness.

I, personally, have had to face great loneliness since Norman passed away in 1993. He was my best friend and we had been married sixty-three years. I've felt a tremendous void in my life as a result and although I'm blessed with a loving and supportive family who live close by, I am still painfully aware that my lifelong companion is not physically by my side. I don't see Norman when I get up in the morning, or hear his laughter in the afternoon, or go for walks with him in the evening. Losing my best earthly friend hurts, but I cannot let this feeling consume me. There are important things left for me to do while I'm still here, projects and friendships that will make Norman smile up in Heaven.

One of the healthiest ways I know of to combat loneliness is to go out of one's way for others. The simple process of thinking of nice things to do for others either in your home, church, or community, is enough to get your mind off your own problems. For example, you could send a member of your church a note expressing your appreciation for him or her. Or you could give a neighbor who has an infant any coupons you receive for baby products. You can also go out of your way for a stranger simply by letting the elderly person in line behind you at the grocery store go ahead. Or you could compliment your pastor or organist after a service. If you look around, you'll discover many ways to extend yourself to others. Caring for others helps lessen your loneliness and reflects your attitudes about God.

Since moving from New York City to Pawling, New York, I have become a part of a wonderful community church that helps me remember these things and provides its members many opportunities to reach out. Because I don't have all the responsibilities I did at Marble Collegiate (which I enjoyed!), Christ Church has been a little more personal for me. Long ago, while the children were growing up, we attended this same church in the summers or when we came up from the city for vacations. I attend it now regularly and particularly enjoy the coffee hour with my friends, who the congregation jokingly call the Merry Widows. Every Easter there are beautiful lilies. The Christ Church Singers delight us with wonderful selections about Christ's Resurrection. This past Easter, the Peale family took up almost three pews because my children, grand-children and their spouses and children came to celebrate together!

I like this church because it's a community church. People from all backgrounds attend it. Virtually every Sunday, I've found it's a community experience with its social hour in the fellowship hall. Christ Church has a wonderful history that has always emphasized family, children and community. As a large urban church, Marble Collegiate had a traditional and formalized worship. Christ Church, though, is a smaller country congregation that draws people from across the valley into a more informal and relaxed approach to worship. People feel comfortable and chat until the first chord of the organ. It's different from Marble but I have happily adapted to it. In fact, one family told me that when they lived in another community for thirteen years, they never quite found a church where they felt comfortable. After a month at our Pawling community church, they were overjoyed that they had found themselves a home!

I know one of the reasons they feel at home is because our pastor always helps us feel spiritually uplifted. But he's also very personally challenging and reminds us of the larger social issues in which Christians can make a difference in the world. One of our outreach programs is for women at the local prison, with whom we do crafts. Sometimes we make midnight runs into the city to feed the homeless. The radio program, too, broadcasts the service throughout the valley so we are often meeting new neighbors or visitors. In other words, church is about—and for—everybody.

As we go into the new millennium, I know that one of the best ways to be aware of God's presence is to commit ourselves to a local church that emphasizes the Bible and positive but simple living. I think church encourages people to discover a sense of community, spiritual support and inspiration that can lead and sustain them in the present and future. Norman once wrote, "Christianity deals with vast realities, but it does so in an uncomplicated way. I have been re-reading the Gospels and letters of Saint Paul. There is where you find out what Christianity really is. Go back to the sources. In my reading, I've noticed that there are four words that stand out. In the New Testament, the word *righteousness* occurs one hundred times; the word *truth,* 120; *life,* 185 times; and *love,* 210 times. The simple teaching of Christian faith is that of righteousness, truth, life, and love. Those are the four words that give us the simple essence of what Jesus taught."

Pretty straightforward, isn't it? If your church reflects these four aspects of Christianity, you've found a good spiritual home!

❧ TAKE IT WITH YOU! ❧

"Find a church that you are comfortable with and begin to look for ways to get involved!"

4

Building a
Marriage
That Moves

Each one of you also must love his wife as he loves himself, and the wife must respect her husband.

—Ephesians 5:33 (NIV)

Two years after I graduated from Syracuse University, I married the most eligible bachelor in town. One blue and gold day in June 1930, I walked down the aisle of the University Church and exchanged vows with Norman. The church was packed because Norman had invited the entire congregation to be a part of our wedding day. Many guests who couldn't get into the sanctuary waited on the lawn outside to greet us after the ceremony. Of course, my father, Rev. Frank B. Stafford, gave me away, and three other reverends, including Norman's father, Dr. Charles Clifford Peale, officiated at the service. The beautiful music, lovely flowers, and all of our family members and friends present made it one of the more special memories I have to this day.

When we walked back down the aisle as husband and wife, Norman's smile spread across his face while his eyes greeted all of the friends, families and parishioners who had come to support us. Then he leaned over, still smiling, and whispered in my ear, "Gee, with this crowd, just think what a collection we could get!" We both laughed, but I knew at that point that I was in for one of the most exciting adventures I would ever have on earth: marriage.

So began a unique and wonderful union for us as Dr. and Mrs. Norman Vincent Peale. I'm so grateful that we learned early on what makes a marriage work, and, maybe more importantly, what makes a marriage last, especially when I think of how the divorce rate in our country has skyrocketed among both religious and non-religious couples since our special June day in 1930. For some time now, I have been concerned about today's staggering statistic of divorce. That is why I hope that by reexamining some important attributes Norman and I learned in our sixty-three years of marriage, perhaps some marriages today could be strengthened.

When I talk about building a marriage that moves, I obviously don't mean one that literally moves apart, dying a slow death in the process. No, a marriage that moves has a double meaning when you think about it: it is a constant adventure, always keeping both spouses moving and growing together in the right direction. But it is also something that also naturally moves or positively influences other people. A marriage that moves, quite simply, is one that helps people grow.

Perhaps that is what is meant by the vow that marriage is "for better or worse." Though I am sure its original meaning included making a commitment that would last in both good and bad circumstances, I wonder if it also meant that marriage tends to bring out the better part of who you are, just as it can also bring out the worst. Norman and I regularly experienced the reality that our marriage kept making us better people, and consequently, we realized that becoming better people kept making our marriage stronger. I think we learned early on how to be flexible with one another. We thrived on discussion—sometimes even in disagreement—and tried to understand each other's needs and nature. Much like the Christian faith, we learned that marriage is an ongoing process that continually demands work. Yet it is also designed to give us rewards of great joy.

That is why, when young people in this day and age ask me about marriage, my first piece of advice to them is to remember that marriage requires love, deep abiding Christian love that survives the changing seasons of romance. Second, I believe it is really important to understand the moods and emotions of your spouse, for that understanding brings an intimacy that keeps the marriage healthy. The third thing I tell them is how important it is to reach an understanding and an agreement, preferably in the beginning of the marriage, about the responsibilities of both husband and wife and how each will respond to their children. Thankfully, there are plenty of churches these days that are offering ministries to help strengthen marriages regarding these issues. That's where support and fellowship becomes a valuable addition to a marriage.

Mostly, however, I believe the key to keeping a marriage moving in the right direction is learning to share similar visions and interests. Norman and I were both interested in the same things and thought along the same lines in so many situations. We both wanted to help people and tried hard to do so, which is, I think, why we were married for more than half a century. Although we were always very busy, I with committees and organizations, Norman with counseling, speaking and heading a large church, we both recognized that our visions were the same.

But we also recognized the unique gifts God had given each of us. In fact, soon after we were married, I discovered that in one respect my husband and I were exactly the opposite. I never had any problem making up my mind about much of anything, but Norman had a hard time making decisions: should he accept this speaking engagement, should he go to this meeting, should we accept or decline this invitation, what emphasis should he make in this speech? Whenever he asked for my advice (which was often), the questions always seemed to come at the most inconvenient times in my well-planned day. But I would stop what I was doing and try to listen patiently. Most of the time he just needed me as a sounding board to help clarify his thinking. And I would go away silently congratulating myself on my patience and understanding, being very glad that the matter was settled.

Many times, to my astonishment, I found the next day that the matter was not settled at all, that he wanted to review it again, that maybe there were angles we had not considered seriously enough. And after another lengthy listening period I would go away realizing his thinking today was almost the opposite to his conclusion of yesterday! Then there were times when plans had been made and I was well along in carrying them out, when suddenly Norman would tell me that something had come up to change them all, that this new opportunity was far more important, and that we weren't going to do what I had thought after all. Talk about a marriage that kept us moving!

Of course, this became a major adjustment for me, a fundamental clash in personal characteristics. What could I do? What should I do? Being absolutely honest with myself, I knew that Norman's response to spontaneity was often best, and that I was too rigid. So I concluded that if God was going to guide our lives I was going to have to keep my mind open so that Norman and

I could use the gifts we had each been given. Norman waited decisions out, and his guidance proved accurate an uncanny number of times. Norman was always helping or encouraging people—yet he didn't really want to go to meetings or run organizations, because he knew those weren't necessarily his greatest gifts. I, on the other hand, would get into an organization and soon find myself president of it, keeping control of the demands of the time and schedules. In other words, we were a partnership, each using and developing our own gifts while moving together in the same direction.

But that was no easy thing. Even up until our last few years together, I still struggled practicing these things. I'd have my plans for the day and suddenly be interrupted by Norman needing to discuss something or wanting to change our schedule. I'd wonder if I'd wasted my time planning. Why couldn't I change my husband's behavior? I even asked myself, do I have to make these adjustments forever?

The answer was a resounding yes, because as human beings, we never stop growing. And as you can guess, our marriage never stopped moving us in the right directions. In fact, if I have developed any real strength of character in my life it is precisely because I realized that only a woman can be a wife, and only a wife can give unique help to her husband. No task was ever as difficult for me to realize as this, but the rewards were—and always will be—tremendous.

I remember once a man came to Norman and told him that after twenty-five years of marriage he was going to leave his wife. My husband asked him the usual questions: Was there deep disagreement that they could not resolve? Was there some other woman in the picture?

No, the man said as he looked at the ground in shame, it was none of these things. There was no quarrel and he was not in love with someone else. Simply put, he was bored, bored beyond all reason, beyond endurance. "While the children were still at home," he confessed to Norman, "my wife had something to do, some purpose in life. But now that they're gone, she has none. She has absolutely no outside interests, no friends, and she talks incessantly—about nothing. She knows nothing about what's happening in the world and, to be honest, I just dread going home after work. I can't stand it much longer."

"Can't you share some of your interests with her?" Norman asked the man, genuinely concerned for his situation. "Can't you draw her into some of your hobbies or interests?"

The man sighed. Then he told my husband that he believed it was too late. "Maybe if we'd started sharing them fifteen years ago, we'd have a chance today. But we didn't. We stayed together because we were raising a family, but we were growing at different rates. Now we're different people, with nothing in common. I'm going to ask her for a divorce." And he did.

This man's marriage had become a ship that was docked in the harbor, not moving in any direction because it wasn't moving at all! To me there is nothing sadder than when two people miss out on the adventure of setting sail in the same direction and sharing the interests, goals and hobbies that puts wind in the sails of their marriage. I learned a long time ago that a simple way to do this was by learning to study your mate. That includes cultivating a willingness to participate, at least occasionally, in activities that interest your spouse more than they might interest you. Of course, some people never learn to do this. For instance, while some women's husbands may be ardent golfers, gardeners or readers, the women they have married make little effort to join them in the areas where they are happiest and where in most cases they would welcome the companionship of their wife. Likewise, some men also may dismiss the interests of their wives as unimportant or irrelevant; they cannot understand why their wives spend time shopping, volunteering at the nursing home or trying new recipes, although most women would welcome their husband's participation in these activities.

I knew a woman who was married to a fanatical trout fisherman. Early each Saturday morning, as her husband prepared to go fishing, she made herself climb out of bed to join him, even though she didn't know a dry fly from a luna moth. At first she was horribly bored, baffled by the intricacies of the sport, sure that she could never acquire even the most rudimentary skill. But gradually her attitude changed. Her husband's enthusiasm was contagious, his delight in teaching her was endearing. In the end, although she never became an expert, she was able to participate with an enthusiasm and enjoyment that at first she would have thought impossible. And it all came about because, wanting to help her relationship with her husband move in the right direction, she enlarged her own horizons.

In a way, this also happened to me. When I was first married, I had no real experience or deep interest in internal church affairs. I knew nothing of board meetings or committee functions. I certainly could not see myself presiding over anything. But it soon became apparent that this was an area where I could be of great support to Norman. Studying him made me realize that this sort of activity was not one of his strong points. Organizational work left him impatient, depleted and restless. Norman was at his best when he was preaching, writing or helping guide an individual through some emotional difficulties. But, ironically, his creativity dried up if anything in the house or his office seemed out of order. As a speaker and writer, his sensitivity—and tension—always seemed to accompany his talents. Norman's practical approach to life and to his vocation grew from an orderly sequence of ideas, and I gradually came to realize that order in his life was essential to his creativity. I began to recognize that if I could take some of the organizational work off his back, go to the committee meetings, report back, summarize, simplify, help Norman make the big decisions and spare him from having to make the little ones, I would be making an enormous contribution. What I didn't initially see then was that this same contribution was one that would also keep his affection, gratitude and esteem for me growing.

So I did it. I studied the organizational structure of the church. I learned how to conduct meetings. I practically memorized Robert's Rules of Order. In the process I made a surprising discovery about myself: I was rather good at this sort of thing! People said that I was actually a good discussion leader with a knack for grasping the essence of a problem, who brushed aside irrelevant detail to get to the point. Consequently, what began as a slightly apprehensive decision to do something useful for Norman became a whole new dimension in my own life, one that expanded steadily throughout the rest of my life. When I look back over our life together as husband and wife, I am astonished and humbled at the opportunities and honors in this field that have come my way. My own listing in *Who's Who in America* has nothing to do with being Norman's wife but represents my own career over nearly seventy years. Thus, when I tell people in this twenty-first century that being a wife is still the greatest career a woman can have, I do it from the vantage point of a successful career woman.

But that doesn't mean a woman shouldn't pursue her own interests or gifts outside of the marriage. The marriage, however, must be the center point for both husband and wife, the first priority and the number one commitment. This then allows both spouses to be fully themselves in creating, with God's help, a fully satisfying marriage that lasts a lifetime.

One of the best ways we found to ensure satisfaction was to schedule into our lives one critical element: fun. That's right, marriages also need fun to keep moving in the right direction. It's astonishing to me that in this age of wonders, young people come up to me and complain that they are bored. Life is so monotonous, they tell me. It's dull, it has lost its flavor, it's just plain boring. I know full well that everyone has their share of unhappiness in this life, and that some people have valid cause to be downhearted. But when the average person complains that he's bored, nine times out ten it's because he isn't making much effort to be anything else. He's not putting any fun into life, which is why he is not getting any out.

Now, more than ever, it seems to me that all important areas of life should be seasoned with fun—marriage, careers, housework, friendships, even our Christian faith. Laughter is one of God's most special gifts to mankind. I love how the Bible tells us over and over to rejoice! And it reminds us that "A merry heart does good like medicine." I remember one Thanksgiving when Norman preached on this topic, as he often liked to do throughout his life. He encouraged the congregation to cultivate a merry heart in all they did, giving thanks to God for the many things that brought them joy. The very next Sunday, one lively young couple responded to his exhortation to let Christianity be fun by putting a well-dried turkey wishbone in the collection plate!

I always felt lucky to be married to such a fun man. Norman's sense of humor and the dramatic, his interest in everything (and I mean everything!), and above all his imagination made him a marvelous companion for people of all ages. When our children were very young, for example, Norman spent hours telling them stories that he made up on the spur of the moment. This generally took place at the dinner table, and the children could hardly wait. Then when they grew up and had children of their own, Norman carried on the story-telling tradition with our grandchildren. That is, if their parents didn't first beat him to it.

I still marvel that for all his popularity and the demands placed on our time in the ministry, we never seemed to lose that sense of fun. If anything, the demands seemed to deepen our marriage, especially as we understood that people could be helped and encouraged to enjoy their personal life, their home life, their parenting and their business life. This reinforced what we felt God wanted us to be, which, in turn, led us to feel more of a sense of responsibility to help people through the church, Norman's books, our various publications and the Peale Center for Christian Living. That very mission amazingly brought us together more frequently, requiring of us a serious sense of humor so we wouldn't feel overwhelmed whenever we'd stop and look at our busy schedules. We learned, in short, to develop an attitude of enjoyment, both together and individually. Sadly, that seems to be a missing ingredient in many marriages today.

Just before Norman's retirement at Marble Collegiate Church, I attended a brunch for members of the congregation. I found myself sitting by a woman from out of town who confessed to me how her husband could have used Norman's sermon on joy that day. I asked her what might be troubling him. She shook her head furiously. "Everything bothers him! The state of the world bothers him, the state of his health bothers him, his job, his finances. He's the most pessimistic man I know. Life in our house with my husband is one long gloom." When I asked the woman why she couldn't change that, she looked at me with total astonishment.

"Why, I'm just his wife. What can I do?" she asked with deep sincerity.

"Everything," I responded as I sipped my tea.

"Oh, come now, Mrs. Peale," she said, half disbelieving and half indignant toward me. "It's easy for you to talk. You're married to one of the world's great optimists. You haven't any idea what I'm up against."

She was right about one thing: Norman was one of the world's great optimists. But she was dead wrong in thinking I didn't understand her situation. For the next twenty minutes or so, we talked through how she might change her marriage as we finished our church brunch. I explained to this woman that I was no exception, that Norman, too, sometimes had his moments of discouragement or depression. (Sometimes, I think he wrote so much about positive thinking because he understood so much about negative thinking!) But I told the woman that fall afternoon that I considered it my job as a wife to understand his moods and do something about it.

This seemed to be a new concept for her. "You almost make it sound as if my husband's pessimism were my fault," she blurted out defensively.

I had to admit that maybe it was. And that in the same way that pessimism was contagious, so, too, was optimism. She probably had a thousand reasons to be thankful to God, from reading an inspiring story to hearing a good sermon to living in a comfortable home. She confessed that there was nothing seriously wrong with her husband's health or finances and that his pessimism was merely a state of mind. When I asked her how she reacted to him, she told me, "He's getting me down. I invite him to shut up."

I went on to share with her my tactic for helping Norman through his darker days by encouraging him to talk it out and unburden himself. As I would listen to him, I'd try to absorb some of his gloominess for him, as if I was made of emotional blotting paper. This tended to shorten the period of depression enormously. She, too, needed to discover her own creative tactics for helping him through his negativism. I explained how the human mind could not hold two sets of ideas simultaneously, so if she helped her husband focus on something good and positive, they could not at the same time dwell on something bad or negative.

As we stood to leave the fellowship hall, the woman

thanked me for our conversation and advice. I encouraged her to try conscientiously for forty days to help her husband have fun and be positive. I said that eventually they'd both find it almost impossible to say anything negative about anybody.

"Why, that's a great idea. But for my husband it may be impossible," she insisted.

"Not if you yourself do some of the things we've talked about," I said to her, walking out of the church and onto the busy city sidewalk. "Not if you really help him. Ask God to guide you and make the best out of each day in your marriage. He will hear your prayer."

I watched that woman walk away that day and I wondered how many other married couples struggled just to have fun or be positive with one another. Since then, I've realized that too few husbands and wives follow some really simple advice to affirm each other, advice my grandmother used to tell me: "If you want a man to keep loving you, you only have to do one thing—appreciate him, and let him know that you do."

Countless times, Grandma's homespun wisdom came in handy for Norman and me. I suspect it would also save a lot of marriages today if more people put it into practice. Of course, it is acceptable to have differences of opinion as long as there is a sense of love, affirmation and appreciation that never leaves the conversations.

And when unrealistic expectations are thrown onto husbands or wives, I am not so sure people these days always know how to discern what is right or important enough to wade through. That's why couples need to encourage each other to grow in their gifts, and enjoy them together.

I'm so glad to see my children do this same thing now in their own marriages. For instance, my daughter's husband John has always encouraged Elizabeth to reach out and pursue the opportunities she's good at. Norman did the same thing with me. But with so much stress and strain put on couples in these busy times, husbands and wives will have to make a conscious effort to get back to the basics of encouragement.

Once a woman came to Norman for counsel, worried because love and enjoyment seemed to be draining out of her marriage. It wasn't that her husband was unfaithful or drank too much or was stingy or jealous. It was just that he never praised her for anything she did, no matter how hard she tried. The wife felt desperate, and wondered how much longer she would last.

Norman asked the husband to come and see him. The big blue-eyed man became defensive when Norman explained the situation.

"This is a lot of nonsense. I love my wife. She knows I love her. Why should I keep telling her all the time?"

He shook his head in confusion.

Norman pressed him, "Is your wife a good housekeeper?"

"Excellent."

"And a good cook?" Norman asked.

"Terrific," the man admitted.

But when Norman asked him the last time he had told her what he thought, he could not remember. Then Norman explained how William James, the great psychologist, wrote a book listing and analyzing all the emotions that motivate and control human behavior. The book was hailed as a masterpiece, but years later James was heard to say ruefully that he had neglected to include the most basic emotion of all: the universal craving for recognition, the deep, unwavering desire in every human heart to be appreciated.

"Now tell me," Norman went on to ask the man, "What do you do for a living?"

He was a manufacturer of electrical appliances, and when Norman asked if they were good appliances, the man assured him they were the best. Then Norman asked him if he was pleased when his customers praised his products, and of course, he confessed that he was.

"A woman who decorates a house, or cooks a fine meal, or serves her community is doing something just as creative as you are doing in manufacturing a good appliance. She needs and deserves praise and recognition just as much as you do. You may have a thousand customers, and so you have a thousand potential sources of appreciation. But your wife probably has only one—and that is you. Because you have failed to grasp this simple truth, your marriage is in danger. But fortunately there is a simple solution."

Now quite concerned, the man was eager to find out what the solution was.

Norman told him to go home from work that very afternoon with flowers for his wife.

"Flowers?" he cried. "She'll think I'm suffering from a guilty conscience. She'll ask me what I've been up to."

"Don't give her a chance to ask questions, "Norman responded. "Hand her the flowers and say, 'These are for you just because you are you.'"

The man finally agreed to carry out these instructions. The next day the wife called Norman and asked if he had prodded her husband into such unheard-of behavior. Norman just laughed and told her that he and her husband had indeed had a talk, and that maybe this was the beginning of a new relationship. From what we heard after that, it was.

Norman knew the right advice to give that man because he had shown appreciation for me a thousand times. From the start of our marriage, we were partners, and talked often about our marriage as a partnership, knowing that our unique gifts contributed to the other's well-being and effectiveness. We'd talk over everything, like where the children went to college since they all went to different schools. Or where the grandchildren went to college or where we should take them on vacation. Or what books to write, which speaking invitations to accept, or what organizational news we needed to know. We never stopped talking with one another. Our ship was always moving! In the process, we always made a point of enjoying and encouraging each other along the way.

⚜ TAKE IT WITH YOU! ⚜

"Find creative ways to encourage and appreciate your spouse and do it! Use your unique gifts to help each other—and your marriage— move in the right direction."

5

Family
Matters

Train a child in the way he should go, and when he is old he will not turn from it.

—Proverbs 22:6 (NIV)

WHEN OUR SON JOHN was a little boy of seven or eight, he had an accident one summer day in which his ear was cut very badly. We rushed him to the hospital where they put him on the operating table. In preparation, they emptied his pockets of all his boyish treasure —marbles and old candies, a pocketknife and bits of string. I can see them to this day and still feel the tug at my heart.

John lay on that table, so pale and helpless, while Norman and I held his hands, which were smudged and dirty from playing. Then Norman thought of all the times he had sent John away from the dinner table with orders to wash his hands, and feeling emotional from seeing his child in such pain, Norman turned to him and said, "Son, I'll never make you go and wash your hands at mealtime again!"

Thankfully, John's ear was patched up with no permanent damage, and the day finally came when John appeared at the dinner table—unwashed! Norman told him to go and wash his hands. But little John fixed his father with a reproachful gaze and responded, "But you *promised*, Dad!" I smiled at the exchange, glad that our son was back to normal and our family was once again discussing a compromise where everyone would be happy.

That's what families do. They care for each other's hurts and then work together to bring out the absolute best in each other. If parenting is about anything, it's about being consistently involved in every aspect of a child's life, knowing that what he or she brings to the family is a special contribution that he or she will eventually give to the world. Family matters are serious business, requiring constant work yet producing an incredible joy that God always intended us to know.

But let me assure you that I do not think family life is necessarily easy. When my children were growing up in the 1940s and 1950s, they sometimes thought I was a little too tough on them. I expected them to come to the dinner table, not in their grubby play clothes but cleaned up and dressed for dinner. They also knew that they would not be excused early either; they had to sit and tell their father and me about their days. And when we made plans for vacations or summer trips, our children always knew they were welcomed and expected to join us.

By showing them consistent love and giving them

proper instruction, we tried very hard to teach our children that not only are there certain matters every family must be concerned with, but that family must always be a priority. It mattered fifty years ago, and it matters now. Especially today, in an age when families seem to be crumbling all around us, when children are starving for parental direction and involvement, I believe there are many time-tested principles that can help knit a family together and train a child for a successful and happy life.

Perhaps it might be easier to distinguish these guidelines into six points, beginning with each letter in the word F-A-M-I-L-Y. (Norman sometimes used this method in his sermons and it seemed to help parishioners remember his message.) First, of all a family needs to be Faithful to one another. Faithfulness acts as a firm foundation so that a family can then nurture Amenable attitudes whenever conflict arises (and it *will* arise!) in order to reach healthy compromises. With these two values firmly in place, meaningful Memories can be built and fostered, which, of course, constantly requires total Involvement in each child's life. When these things work together, Loving interactions with one another take place. Joined together, these five attributes (Faithfulness, Amenability, Memories, Involvement, Love) create what I like to call a Yes-focus, a positive perspective that helps nurture a joyful Christian approach to life. I hope the following helps explain why these F-A-M-I-L-Y matters are so important.

First of all, if parents model to their children a commitment (or faithfulness) to each other and to family times, the children will naturally understand that this is what they should do too. Regardless of how busy someone's schedule becomes, it is imperative that members of a family remain faithfully available to one another if they want to develop a sense of trust and unity, because when they do, they also are creating a shield that protects them from the challenges and temptations the world will likely throw their way.

Faithfulness to family requires a firm decision to build supportive relationships with one another. Of course, this can occur in any number of ways, from fun outings and trips to simple conversations. Sometimes, it happens when you least expect it. When Norman and I were married in 1930, I hadn't yet realized just how seriously his family took their commitment to one another. After our wedding, we were to drive to the Adirondack Mountains of New York to stay in a little cabin and enjoy some rest. But Norman had been scheduled to make a speech a week later at the baccalaureate ceremony of Cazenovia Seminary, where his younger brother Leonard was a member of the graduating class. His parents,

Clifford and Anna Peale, would be driving all the way from Ohio to attend the graduation ceremony, so Norman asked me why they could not come along on our honeymoon and share the cabin. It had several rooms, he explained; his parents could have a vacation while we had our honeymoon. (Remember, this was 1930!) I wondered at first if he was joking.

He was not, I quickly learned. And because I was determined to get along with my new in-laws, I made no objections to their accompanying us, although I have to admit that at first I was a little sad about the decision. I had wanted to be alone with my husband. Still, I knew how important family was to him. So on Monday, we packed up two cars and drove to the mountains—with the Peale family.

Once I accepted the concept of a somewhat crowded honeymoon, everything went smoothly—until we all realized that the cabin was a little more isolated than any of us had expected. It stood far back in a wilderness that we quickly imagined to be populated with wolves, bears, escaped lunatics, runaway criminals and all sorts of other dreadful menaces. One evening, as darkness was falling, Norman told me he heard an ominous scratching sound on the porch. He snatched up a hatchet, gritted his teeth and flung wide the door.

There sat a little chipmunk, looking almost as frightened as I did! We laughed at the silliness of our unfounded fears and enjoyed the rest of the week together. When we left for Leonard's graduation, I was glad to have gotten to know my in-laws a little better, although I was ready to start a family of our own with Norman. Through the years, we joked about how the honeymoon prepared us to live a full and faithful family life, even if it was a little more full and faithful than I might have liked at that point!

If members of a family understand one another's commitment, it makes it a lot easier to be <u>A</u>menable whenever conflicts occur. Most young parents will find, as they grow older and wiser, that they can almost never change objectionable or undesirable characteristics in their spouses or children by frontal assault. Angry recriminations just make matters worse. The only approach that works is a calm rational discussion, an appeal to fair-mindedness, or a quiet demonstration of how hurtful or unwise the negative or objectionable quality really is.

I remember one young woman—I'll call her Mrs. Harrison—who married into a very close-knit family. They were not only very fond of one another, they were all great talkers. Whenever there was a Harrison family gathering, this combination of affection and fluency became overwhelming. Nobody else could get a word in edgewise. Guests just had to sit there, mute and helpless. The members of the family were so interested in one another, and in family activities, anecdotes, jokes and reminiscences, that the rest of the world and the people in it didn't seem to exist for them.

Some new wives might have accepted this situation with resignation. Some might have smoldered in silence. But this was a forthright young woman, so she decided to take it up with her husband. "Darling," she said (which is always a good word to start with!), "I don't think any of you realize it, but when you Harrisons get together you're really quite rude. You don't show even polite interest in what anyone outside the family might have to say. You just turn them off."

The husband was not so easily convinced. "You're being hypersensitive, aren't you? You know perfectly well we're always delighted to hear anything you have to say. All you have to do is speak up!" He smiled as he spoke with his wife.

"I do try to speak up," she responded. "And I've heard other people try. But it's hopeless. If we attempt to tell a story, one of you always tops it with one of your own. Or else it reminds you of some family episode that you just have to tell about. And the worst of it is that you're not even aware you're doing it."

The husband told her he still thought she was exaggerating and cheerfully proclaimed, "We can't be as bad as that."

The young wife said no more, but went out and bought a small battery-powered tape recorder. At the next Harrison family gathering, she hid the machine in one of the compartments of the sideboard and recorded the whole dinner-table conversation. That night, when she and her husband were back home and the children had gone to sleep, she played the tape, stopping it occasionally gently to offer her own comments. ("Now here's Jim's wife trying feebly to talk about her own college days. Notice how your mother cuts her off." Or, "This is me, trying to speak up the way you told me I should. See how far I got!")

The husband, utterly amazed, called a family conference of his parents and siblings and played the tape for them, adding some of the comments his wife had made. Everyone was astounded. Fortunately, being a warmhearted, faithful and amenable family, they took no offense but honestly tried to mend their ways. Most of the time, my friend told me, they succeeded.

Discussions like this are the best choice to resolving conflict. But sometimes a sharp quarrel that clears the air is better than a sullen deadlock that drags on and on. I certainly don't want to imply that a bitter argument is always a good thing. People say and do things in anger that can damage any relationship, sometimes permanently, and parents especially need to be careful in how they discuss things with children who are already sensitive and easily shattered. But I do think that a disagreement between married partners can actually be constructive and useful if (and it's a big *if*) it's handled in the right way. Children in turn will learn how to handle conflict in a healthy positive way.

Over the years, there were plenty of areas where Norman and I were not in accord. I wouldn't think of agreeing with him on every subject! Diversity is so much more interesting. But we did learn certain dos and don'ts that tended to turn potential arguments into useful discussions.

One, for example, was the importance of easing up gradually on the area of disagreement, taking just a piece of it at first (the least explosive piece), discussing that aspect, then letting the matter rest for a while. We found that if you nibble around the edges of an argument, instead of trying to bite off more than any of you can chew, you're likely to be able to digest the problem much better in the end. I heard a successful business executive say once that when a touchy subject had to be dealt with in her board room, she tried to make sure that the discussion was conducted in slow motion. That's a pretty good rule for family discussions as well.

Another amenable technique that I have learned to value is simply the practice of silence at certain times. There are times in arguments when you suddenly realize that the other person is no longer talking about the issue at hand, but about something else that is highly charged with emotion. (Teenagers are notorious for this.) When this happens, the best thing to do is not to argue or counterpunch, but just let the other person talk himself out. As the old saying goes, silence is golden.

There are various other common-sense approaches that can take the sting out of marital or family dis-agreements if we can keep them in mind: the impor-tance of compromise; the value of emphasizing the positive when making your case; the trick of trying—really trying—to put yourself in the other's shoes and seeing the issue from his or her point of view. All of these guidelines for keeping a faithful family amenable are helpful and probably obvious, but I'm still surprised how many families have never thought of them or tried to apply them. When disagreements arise, they react with anger and then again with more anger. But when there is a healthy commitment to working things through, everyone benefits.

Perhaps no place are these techniques better tested than in the making of memories, and in particular when families travel together. Memories help shape a child's values and esteem, and any creative attempt to build them is a parent's best tool. That's probably why Norman and I spent much time, resources and energy in giving our children as many opportunities to explore the world as we could. Each summer when they were old enough, they attended camp in Vermont or Maine. Often, we'd bring them up from the hustling pace of New York City to the small country town of Pawling or to a mountain lake to enjoy nature together. I'm encouraged by how much they've applied this value in raising their own children; consequently, our grandchildren have also experienced many wonderful opportunities. Building meaningful memories is a great way to keep a family strong, even as the children grow older and become parents themselves.

That's why Norman and I enjoyed a marvelous trip with our children and grandchildren to the Holy Land for Christmas in 1968. Like thousands of other Christian pilgrims, we walked together on the roads and hillsides where Christ our Lord had walked two thousand years before. Norman and I believed that such a trip would build an unforgettable memory that would encourage our family in their Christian faith for years to come. We felt that to travel together to such holy places over Christmas would be deeply meaningful.

So seventeen of us, ranging in ages from twelve to

seventy (Norman was the oldest), packed our suitcases and flew to Jordan. At the time, I was vice-chairman of the executive committee of the American Bible Society, and I gave each family member an identical copy of the King James Version of the Bible as well as marking pens and a personal journal. We all agreed to record our thoughts and reactions as we toured the lands of the Bible. Then I gave assignments to various family members: our oldest daughter Maggie and her husband, Rev. Paul Everett, prepared and led our daily spiritual gatherings; our son John (who's a college professor) and his wife Lydia kept us abreast of relevant Scriptures as they related to each place we traveled; and our daughter Liz and her husband, John Allen, carried our money and handled all the bills. Even our grandchildren offered their unique contributions by reading Scriptures aloud or leading us in singing as we traveled.

We went by bus or horseback through mountains and valleys, beside lakes and villages, enjoying the sights of these biblical lands. Every night, after a full day of visiting caves or hillsides or town markets, we'd gather in our hotel room for a prayer meeting to give thanks for the blessing of having this spiritual experience together. The few chairs available in our room were occupied by the older folks, while the rest sat on beds or floor, but no one seemed to mind; we all were aware of a strong sense of family love and unity along the way. And when Liz and John's daughters, Rebecca and Katie, returned to high school in Connecticut, their classmates were amazed that they had traveled for two weeks with seventeen family members! But our girls simply responded to their friends, "We love each other. It's fun when we're together."

I still remember our last night together in Israel when Norman gathered the children and grandchildren, looked straight into their eyes, and said, "You're all good, honorable, Christian young people and we, your grandparents and parents, think you're great. We know you'll always walk in the footsteps we've been trying to follow." That trip, like so many others we were able to take through the years, helped bring our family closer together and deepened our unity and closeness between each other. And it also strengthened our Christian faith, being profoundly affected by the surroundings of Jerusalem and Bethlehem at Christmas.

But that's what the adventure of making memories like this will do: in addition to enjoying new sights, meeting people of different nations, eating new foods, and being inspired by walking where Jesus walked, we grew together as a family. It was such a good experience that seven years later, when Norman was almost seventy-seven years old, we decided to take the entire family on another Christmas trip: this time though it would be to Africa for a safari!

The Samburu Game Park in Kenya was far away from our usual New York Christmas traditions. Norman and I shared a tent pitched near a fast-flowing brown river. Our children and grandchildren were in tents on either side. The heat and dust and burning sun seemed an unusual contrast to the decorated windows and huge Christmas tree of Rockefeller Center we typically saw, or to the roads of Bethlehem we'd visited seven years before. At night the African forest resounded with barks, screeches, splashes and, once, just behind our tents, a grunting sound that we discovered the next day had probably been made by a leopard. I went outside one night and saw a guard with his rifle over his shoulder. When I asked him what he was doing, he said he was protecting us from wolves.

On Christmas Eve, we enjoyed a splendid day of viewing animals. We saw a beautiful herd of zebras, seventy-six elephants (the grandchildren counted), a cheetah chasing an impala, and a nursing lioness, all magnificent in their natural surroundings. Then it was time for a shower before our Christmas Eve dinner, which was also a bit of an adventure. The camp helpers heated water, put it in a bucket, then hoisted the bucket to the top of a pole behind a tent. From there the water ran down a pipe into the rear of the tent where, standing on slats, the bather could soap and rinse himself off.

We had been told the evening's dinner would be a special one. When we entered the eating tent I noticed a straggly brown bush had been set up, and decorated with small colored lights and some tinsel and red ribbon. Then we were called to the edge of the river, where chairs had been set up for all of us so that we could see the opposite bank, where two herders were guarding their cattle, their spear tips gleaming like points of light in the gathering dusk. At the peaceful, timeless sight, we knew that these herders and their charges had not changed in thousands of years. They belonged to their landscape just as the shepherds on the hills outside Bethlehem had belonged to theirs.

At that moment, one of our grandchildren began to sing, tentatively at first, "O Little Town of Bethlehem." Gradually others joined in and then we sang "Hark! The Herald Angels Sing" and "Joy to the World." Someone read the immortal Christmas story from Luke: "And there were in the same country shepherds abiding in the field, keeping watch over their flock by night." Norman and I looked at the faces of our descendants, singing songs, sharing feelings that in a very real way went back almost two thousand years to that simple manger in a simple town, with the herders standing by in a parched and primitive land.

Far away from the bright lights and packages of our traditional Christmases in New York, we experienced a new kind of Christmas, and in the process, created a memory that has both sustained and unified our family ever since. I realize that not every family has the means nor the time to travel together around places like Africa or the Holy Land. But long before we set out to travel, we discovered dozens of creative ways to build memories for a family. And I'm convinced that with a strong sense of heritage, of history and of special memories, a child will take with him a healthy self concept as he enters adulthood.

Taking trips together—whether across town or across the world—convinced us that the only way our children could understand the world was to experience it. We had always wanted them to be aware of the wonderfully different races, cultures and languages throughout the world. We always tried to go to interesting places, and I'd read about where we were going beforehand to prepare the family for what to expect.   Recently both of my daughters told me what a gift it had been to be able to travel. It was a terrific bonding experience for all of us to be together: in the earlier days, with just the immediate family, then traveling with the spouses and their children who were building friendships with their cousins. Now, our grandchildren want their parents to take them to Africa!

Part of this commitment to making memories requires a total Involvement in building supportive relationships. That's why we went to every child's and grandchild's graduation ceremony from college, just to be together while encouraging the special graduate. And Norman and I invited our entire family to help us celebrate our fiftieth wedding anniversary in Interlacken, Switzerland. We traveled by train and by bus around Switzerland with all of them, through the beautiful Alps and to other places in Europe like Salzburg, Austria, where *The Sound of Music* was filmed. We even visited a World War II concentration camp in Germany—Dachau. Each provided an enriching experience for us personally and as a family.

To this day, we still go to Mohonk, New York, to visit the beautiful mountain lake there and the old rambling Quaker hotel with rocking chairs on the porch. Norman and I often took the children there when they were growing up, and it was the glorious site where we celebrated Norman's ninety-fourth birthday in 1992!

Whether it was summer camp, train trips across the country, mountain visits or walks through a local park, meaningful memories have always been one of the greatest ways our family has grown together—and stayed involved with one another. I believe such experiences help children build bridges across cultures and careers once they become adults, providing them with the confidence and exposure to make a positive contribution to their own communities, families, and country.

I always tried to stay as involved in my children's lives as I could. How? I'd ask them to give me their college schedules so I could pray for them when they had exams. I attended dozens of Christmas pageants over the years, and if they had a basketball game or some other event, Norman and I always prayed for our children and tried to attend each. We were bonded by prayer because family was a priority for us.

Our children always ate with Norman and me; they weren't fed early by a maid, for we didn't have one. In those days schedules weren't what they are today, when soccer practice and work and a million other things can often intrude. Perhaps we need to return to the idea of making meals a time for conversation and ideas. I remember how Norman would go around the dinner table and ask each of the children what fun thing they had done that day. Eagerly, they'd tell about the relationships or arguments they had, or games they played at school.

Even if meal time doesn't work, families need to be creative in planning time together. If the family plays a sport or does an activity together, that will help strength-en their closeness. I've seen this happen as my children have raised their children and tried to institute a special time over a meal, even though the grandchildren initial-ly resisted, claiming their friends didn't have to sit at the dinner table with their parents. But when those same friends come over, they love staying for hours around the table talking. They recognize that a parent's involvement in their lives is a treasured thing, one that leads to lov-ing relationships.

Once when Rev. Billy Graham came to Madison Square Garden in New York City in the 1950s, he asked Norman to be on the platform with him. I sat in the bal-cony with Ruth Graham and we had a good time dis-cussing the challenges we faced with raising our children. We both felt a responsibility to be at the cru-sade for our husbands when they needed us. And I had been involved in helping organize prayer cells around the New York area to pray for the success of the crusade. Consequently, I had gotten in touch with a lot of church-es and helped them form small groups in homes to pray for this outreach. Ruth and I both knew these home groups were important for families throughout the city.

As a result, our children saw our love for Christ in working together with other churches. But long before Ruth and Billy came to New York, our children also saw through our family times and involvement how we loved them no matter what happened through the day. I know love may seem like an obvious quality in keeping a family together, but many people today tend to overlook this. They assume their children know they love them by the things they buy for them, or the money they give them, when in reality, all children really want is to hear their parents tell them "I love you" or to see their affection in spending time together. The Bible says that the "greatest of these is love" and in a family atmosphere, there is certainly no greater glue that holds relationships together than love.

Yet the Bible also says that "We love because God first loved us." I believe that a parent's love for God is a marvelous gift to give her children. That is why a parent's personal faith should never stop growing. And though it might seem obvious to many of us that a strong Christian family is loving, I doubt this can be emphasized enough. Children need to know they are loved through consistent actions that back up what they hear from their parents. Siblings need to learn to love each other, and parents can never get tired of hearing that their children love them. In short, all of us can only thrive when we are certain of the love of God and of those closest to us. When this is neglected, or when pride gets in the way, everyone misses out. But when

God's love directs us, we share a love that binds us together in wonderful ways.

It's no secret that my husband suffered all his life from what we call today an inferiority complex. This always baffled me, because I saw him as an extremely talented and sensitive man whose gifts translated well into his life as a preacher, counselor, father, husband and friend. Still, whether speaking before thousands at a conference or preaching to a New York City crowd, Norman was not very confident in what he did. Often, he was criticized by other ministers, which was very difficult for him. So I found myself trying hard to encourage him to keep using his gifts no matter what his critics said, since so many people seemed to benefit from his insights and faith.

When Norman began writing some of his first books, he felt like a failure. In one in particular, he tried to explain the principles of Christianity in easy-to-understand language for ordinary folks. The entire manuscript discussed simple techniques from the Bible that encouraged people to renew their attitudes by being thankful and by searching the Scriptures for powerful verses of faith. It explained the ABC's of Christianity, helping readers understand the principles of happiness and success. But once he re-read the pages he had written, he walked over to the wastebasket and dropped them all in. He was certain it was no good and that no publisher would be interested.

I found it there the next day, began reading it and quickly realized that Norman was wrong in his assessment of its potential. What I read was a helpful and practical approach to Christian living. I cleaned it up and sent it to a publisher we knew. Not long after that, he contacted Norman about wanting to publish it. It was called *A Guide to Confident Living,* and in the next four years, it went through twenty-five more printings.

It was a very readable book, projecting the same crispness and authority that Norman had in the pulpit. The message was one that he had been preaching for years—that with God's help, you can do anything. Only now the illustrations were sharper, the psychological insights were clearer, and the practical how-to-do-it aspects were plainer. Simply put, Norman conveyed that Christianity wasn't vague or impractical, but instead offered a specific set of principles that would give an individual great power over his own thoughts and emotions, and hence over his environment. If a person, he said, would believe in the reality and goodness of God, submit to His will and surrender his life to Jesus Christ, then an inner peace would come to him that would greatly aid in the solution of all problems.

Apparently, it worked, because he then went on to

publish several more books, one of which, *The Power of Positive Thinking,* has remained in print to this day. Norman always called his books, "God-help books, not self-help books." And he was right. Even though he always struggled with staying positive about himself, he never tired of saying Yes! to God.

I'm glad I retrieved that manuscript that day, because it has provided so much encouragement for countless people. And whenever someone walked up to Norman and thanked him for writing his books, he, too, was encouraged.

That's what happens when we stay Yes! Not only are others encouraged by our positive attitudes, but we also receive it back from them. Being positive is contagious, and so when a family is able to support each other, anchored in the promises of God, they can count on it coming back to them in a variety of wonderful ways!

❧ TAKE IT WITH YOU! ❧

"Recall the six attributes for being a F-A-M-I-L-Y and talk about how to incorporate them into your own family!"

Photo

Album

1907-"My father and me before my first birthday, in Iowa."

1908-"*Family Portrait on a trip to Canada where my parents, were from. (l-r: Charles, Loretta, Frank and Ruth).*"

c.1920's-"As a teenager at Northwestern high school in Detroit."

June 20, 1930-*"Leaving steps of University Methodist Church of Syracuse, NY. This is the first picture as husband/wife. Norman's brother Bob and my sister-in-law Eleanor are with us."*

1931-"Rev. Stafford and his musical family-mother played beautifully and often we performed family concerts in churches where they could take pictures. (l-r: Loretta, Ruth, Frank, Charles and William)."

Mid 1940's-"Plowing up the ground in Pawling."

1948- *"1st home in Pawling, Sugar Tree Farm,*
Dr. Peale always pointing the way."

1948- *"On the farm in*
Pawling. We're
exploring nature
here—or at least
a chicken."

1954-"Dr. and Mrs. Peale with Dale Evans."

1954-"We're on the T.V. set of 'This is Your Life,' Maggie is 21 here, Liz 12, and John is 18."

April 1, 1954-
"Frequently got my
portrait taken for
speaking, etc."

November 17, 1957-
"Interchurch Center
groundbreaking ceremony."

Late 1950's-"Norman and I with subscriber plates at Foundation for Christian Living. We used to address envelopes with these plates."

1961- "Margaret is getting ready for her wedding at Marble Collegiate Church in New York City. She married Paul F. Everett."

1962-"Filming of 'One Man's Way'-the story of Dr. Peale, released in 1962 starring Don Murray and Diana Highland."

1963-"Mrs. Peale at 100th anniversary of Red Cross."

1969- "Madame & Sir Chiang Kai-shek with the Peales in Taiwan outside their home."

1971- "Christmas 1971-Margaret (Peale) and Paul Everett with Jennifer and Chris."

1971-"Christmas 1971-John and Lydia Peale with Laura, Clifford, and Lacy."

1971-"Christmas 1971-Elizabeth (Peale) and John Allen, with Rebecca and Katie."

1972-"Mrs. Peale receiving one of four honorary degrees. 1972 Webber College."

1973- "Dr. and Mrs. Peale with Stanley Kresge, personal friend and business man (K-Mart), at Hope College, 1973."

Mid 1970's- "Making Christmas cookies at our home in Pawling with Rebecca 4, and Katie 3."

Late 1970's- "The whole family with grandchildren."

1984-"Norman Vincent Peale and Ruth Stafford Peale with Pope John Paul II in Rome."

6

The Joy
of Service

"Whoever wants to become great among you must be your servant...just as the Son of Man did not come to be served, but to serve, and to give his life as a ransom for many."

—MATTHEW 20:26, 28 (NIV)

N OT LONG AGO, I was going through some old files and came across a most inspiring story I had clipped from the newspaper. It went something like this:

> *At forty-one, Stanley Gould easily could have excused himself from trying to reach his potential. Cerebral palsy had caused his limbs to twist and his speech to slur. But instead of lying back and doing nothing, he filled in as a volunteer assistant basketball coach at the local school. He was so good at what he did that when the school's head coach resigned, Stanley was able to fill the position. Then, along with coaching, he began helping out in the school's computer lab. And when the local library needed board members, Stanley volunteered again.*
>
> *This is a perfect example of a man who is constantly broadening his horizons to achieve his potential. And although he is wheelchair-bound, his spirit is not bound to anything. "It's all for*

the kids," he told one reporter. "I can stay home
and feel sorry for myself, or I can be active and
happy."

The story went on to say how the school principal believed Stanley had an uncanny ability to counsel young people; if they knew he could do difficult things, they could too. He was not only a great role model, but he also gave these young people the drive they needed to continue on with life. Why did he do it? Because he opened himself up to new experiences. In the process, he uncovered his potential and positively touched the lives of those around him.

Stanley's life is one of the best examples I've heard of defining what Christian service should be. I have always believed that the primary way we can get more out of life and unleash our potential is to serve. Today, many communities literally could not function without the faithful efforts of volunteers serving in roles such as teacher's aides, hospital chaplains, Little League coaches and in civic organizations. There are a thousand different ways we can serve our communities, but probably only a few different reasons why we should.

Serving not only enhances your personality, it makes you think about the different circumstances people go through, and it tends to organize your life since you have to be committed. At the heart of the Christian faith is a deep sense of serving God by serving each other. Simply put, it's a responsibility of our Christian faith to help meet the needs of those around us. The more we grow in our Christian faith, the more likely we are to want to serve. Of course, some people will understand those needs better than others. But regardless of how we're gifted, I believe everyone can experience the deep joy that comes from giving of yourself to the betterment of others.

On my desk I've had a golden plaque that has the Golden Rule written across it, and throughout my life, I've tried hard to fulfill it: "Love one another as you love yourself." Whether it's speaking to a women's group, working on a committee for an organization I've believed in or attending my grandchildren's musical recitals, I have always tried to consider how I would want others to respond to me as I seek to serve them. As a result, I have learned through the years that if you're going to accomplish anything by serving, you have to have a genuine motivation to want to do it. Then you have to spend time and thought in order to do it well. With God's help and with the Golden Rule as your guide, it doesn't take long to discover the magnificent joy that comes in a simple act of giving.

As Norman and I discovered more opportunities to serve and the more we were able to travel around the country, the more we saw how we could better serve others. For instance, we always wanted to help ministers be more effective in their own churches. So we created the School for Practical Christianity, where pastors and their spouses could come twice a year for workshops and lectures. For close to twenty years, we held a variety of workshops on topics such as prayer, parenting, recruiting volunteers and conflict resolution. Many times, though, we just let people talk freely about their pastoral experiences, and encouraged them to learn from one another throughout the sessions.

Eventually we discovered a wonderful and simple key to joyful Christian service that we have since passed on to others: "Find a need and fill it." We were always asking each other, "What are the needs out there and how can we fill them?" Then we'd ask our church staff the same thing. Or we'd ask the pastors at our retreats. And because Norman's sermons were always very people-oriented, we often found ourselves wondering how they could meet the varied needs of our growing congregation in New York, one of the most diverse cities in the world. Quickly, we also saw that serving others doesn't have to be organizationally based; it's an attitude that comes when you are willing to take a look at your own gifts.

At a dinner party some years ago, I found myself sitting next to a well-known novelist. During the evening, someone came over to our table and complimented him on his ability to portray life exactly the way it is.

The writer smiled and shook his head. "That," he said to his admirer, "is exactly what I don't do. If I simply held up a mirror to life, nobody would be very interested, because anyone can observe what goes on around him. No, what a novelist tries to do is rearrange life. Life is the raw material. We reshape it so that it becomes more understandable and believable. Sometimes we give it a happy ending; sometimes not. In general, we try to portray life so that it makes a point—and that's what the craft of fiction is all about."

Throughout the years, as Norman and I (and others now at the Peale Center for Christian Living) listened to people with difficult personal needs and problems, we thought how wonderful it would be if, like the novelist, we could rearrange their lives and guarantee them happy endings. Obviously, the raw material of real life can't be shaped so easily. It demonstrates the inescapable fact that the world is full of trouble and need, and everyone will have his share sooner or later. But we have always tried to point out that the world is also full of stories that show how someone overcame trouble or met someone's need. We've been quick to emphasize that the twisted strands and tangled threads of people's lives *can* be straightened out—with God's help. And that trouble *can* be overcome because life is worth living in spite of the blows it deals. Sometimes we point out that partial solutions have to be accepted while one waits, with patience, for the final plan to unfold.

While this business of trying to help and serve needy, troubled people has never been easy, it remains one of the most fascinating and rewarding aspects of our lives as Christians. One of the main reasons is because so much good comes about when we're willing to find a need and fill it.

One such example is the time I met a pretty woman in her mid-thirties, quietly dressed, with ash blonde hair and unhappy, dark brown eyes. As I walked toward her in our church office, she told me, with a faint smile of resignation, that she didn't think I could help her with her trouble. But she had asked for an interview with me anyway. Her problem and need turned out to be poignantly simple: She loved her husband yet he had died the year before.

A sudden heart attack had killed him twelve months ago, she told me, without warning to anyone. Her healthy, lovely husband was gone in what seemed an instant, and she had not been able to recover from the loss. After the initial grief and shock were over, his widow went back to her job as a receptionist in a doctor's office. She had tried desperately, she said, to make some sort of adjustment, to achieve some sort of acceptance. But her life was one long ache of loneliness.

They had had no children, which had drawn them even closer together. She had a mother and a sister, but they lived in a distant city. She had the usual number of friends—all of whom were kind, but who also, she said resignedly, tended to forget a widow when it came to making plans for parties or get-togethers.

I asked if she had gone out at all with other men since her husband's death.

Yes, she told me, a few times. But it was difficult. Most men apparently thought that a widow would be sex-starved and available. "I may be sex-starved," she said wryly. "In fact, I know I am. But I am not available. You see, I happen to have some standards and I'm still in love with Jim. That rules out any other man for me."

When I asked her if she thought remarriage were a possibility for her, she admitted that it could be. "But," she went on, "I don't think much of widows who rush around trying to catch a man whether they're in love with him or not."

"Of course," I said slowly, "but perhaps you're being a little too defensive about all this. Perhaps unconsciously you feel that your late husband wouldn't want you to remarry."

She made a little gesture of helplessness. "It's not really remarriage that I worry about. It's this lost feeling, this terrible emptiness. It's as if part of me had been cut away."

"That's understandable," I said. "A part of you has been cut away, temporarily at least." Then the young woman put her clenched fists suddenly up to her temples. "I hate it," she said in a choked voice. "I hate being alone. I hate being a widow!"

"Why don't you stop applying that word to yourself?" I said to her softly. "It's loaded with all sorts of gloomy connotations. When you keep calling yourself a widow, you're almost labeling yourself a has-been. Why not think of yourself as a single, unmarried person, with the emphasis on that last word. You're still a person, with all the unique qualities that made your husband love you and your friends admire you. If you're working in a doctor's office, you're still serving a very useful function. You're helping people. You're pulling your weight in the boat."

She confessed that the daytime hours were not so bad but that going home alone and knowing no one was there was "so different from what . . . from what . . . " She could not go on. I felt badly for her.

99

"I know, because I've heard that same thing from other women who have lost their husbands," I told her. "The hours between five P.M. and seven P.M. are somehow the worst." She could see that I understood some of her pain and genuinely wanted to help, so she asked me what I would do if ever I found myself in her shoes.

I thought for a long, silent moment about what I would be like if I had lost Norman at so young an age. Then I turned to her and responded, "I think I would tell myself that some loneliness is inevitable, but I need to tighten my belt and try to hold on. I think I'd be as natural and normal as I possibly could. I'd look for new interests. I might take up some special project that would force me to get out of the house and make contact with other people. For example, I might ask the Federation of Women's Clubs if they could use me as a speaker. I'd entertain a great deal more than I do now, and I'd try to include people who are lonely. Above all I'd keep telling myself that the separation from the person I love most was only temporary, and that some day, as the Bible promises, I would see him again."

She nodded slowly. Then she told me that she often tried to remember that promise now, but on some days it still wasn't enough to help her through.

I continued, "There's only one answer to your problem right now. You have to make up your mind not to give in to grief or to loneliness. You must keep going and pray. You also have to face up to the fact that sometimes, if it's prolonged beyond a certain point, grief can become a self-centered thing."

Then I remembered a woman Norman had met one day in the lobby of a local hotel and shared her story with this young widow: Norman was going to a Rotary Club luncheon, and happened to see a woman sitting forlornly in the lobby. He recognized her as the wife of a former Rotarian who had died a few months before. He approached her and asked what she was doing there. She told him—with tears—that ever since her husband's death she had come to the hotel every Thursday when the Rotary Club met. She would sit in the lobby and think about her husband, shed a few tears and finally go home.

Norman asked her to wait until the luncheon was over so they could talk some more, and she agreed. He then spoke to her kindly but bluntly. He felt what she was doing was somewhat morbid and depressing, and that her husband—who had been a jovial, outgoing man—would be the first to disapprove. He asked her what she was doing with herself aside from sitting around grieving. When she admitted that she was doing little or nothing, he took her down to Marble

Collegiate Church where a group of volunteers was busy mailing out booklets of inspirational material.

"Put this lady to work," he said to the volunteer in charge, "and when she's done whatever you give her to do, think of something else to keep her busy!" In the end, he helped the woman find a permanent position as an unpaid volunteer in a large charitable organization and gradually—because she began thinking about others instead of herself—she was able to find peace of mind, a degree of contentment and the joy of service.

I turned to the woman I had just been talking with and encouraged her to consider doing the same thing. "Don't brood about the past or worry about the future. Time is on your side, because it does heal wounds and bring new opportunities for living. You're young and attractive. I feel sure that God has great plans for your life if you'll just trust Him and be patient."

The young woman walked out of our office with a wonderful smile on her face. I do not know if she took my advice or not, but I do know that a certain level of personal healing and joy waited for her if she would be willing to reach out to others in need.

Year after year, our family would run into people with difficulties, sorrows, problems or great needs. Almost all of them were lovable, appealing human beings. Sometimes Norman or I could help, sometimes we could not. But we put them all in God's hands. Today more than ever, I believe the challenge has not grown stale: To serve God by trying to serve people lies at the heart of all true happiness.

Once, I was asked at a ladies' luncheon what made me happy. I told my audience that there was no absolutely foolproof formula for happiness. Then I encouraged them to stop struggling to be happy, since happiness isn't something you can deliberately set out to achieve for yourself, like skill at typing or a college degree. In fact, the more you focus on your own happiness, or lack of it, the more it will continue to elude you. This is because preoccupation with self is the enemy of happiness. The more concerned you are with your own pleasures and successes—or your own problems and failures for that matter—the less contented you are going to be.

In terms of deep down happiness, I told these women, nothing compares to volunteer work in a local hospital, leading a Girl Scout troop, or helping a less fortunate person in some direct and personal way. Then I asked them how many such outlets they had in their lives at that moment. And I encouraged them to consider the fact that if they'd double them, they would then quadruple their chances for obtaining this thing called happiness!

The point is that we touch another's life by visiting the sick or tutoring a child or helping at the homeless shelter or volunteering in our local church. Norman and I have always been proud of the fact that our children grew up to be adults who also looked for opportunities to serve their community. Today, Liz is on the executive boards of several community organizations. Maggie has led countless Bible studies in her home, and John often finds ways to serve on the college campus where he teaches.

And our children's spouses have also found the secret to joyful living. For instance, John's wife Lydia is always volunteering at an AIDS clinic, or tutoring a child in an after-school program. My son-in-law John looks at service as a way of gratitude, which is the healthiest emotion. He looks for creative ways to serve, whether it's through street theatre or sending urban kids to college. And my other son-in-law, Paul, has volunteered his time on several committees and boards.

If you do your homework and have some good ideas, everyone can discover the joy of service. But where do we begin to find what we can give? At home, of course. As a young wife, I thought Norman's sermons could and should be distributed to others who might not have been able to hear him on Sunday mornings from the pulpit. So for our first few years in ministry, our kitchen table became the place where I began to edit his sermons, and then wrote an address on each one. I worked hard to put the spoken word into print, because I was certain others would get something from it. Soon, our mailing list grew beyond what I could handle alone. But I firmly believed that the hours I spent on those early sermons and materials would make a difference, somehow, somewhere, in someone's life.

One day, Norman returned home from a business trip to Chicago; he was so excited that he could barely wait to tell me what had happened on his trip. Apparently, he was walking out of a restaurant to catch a cab to the airport when one of the waitresses hurried after him in her uniform. She rushed up to Norman, tapped him on the shoulder and cried, "Oh, Dr. Peale, I just love you!"

"Well," laughed Norman, "I love you, too. But what has happened to make us love each other so much?"

"I'll tell you," she answered. "I have a little boy. His father left us soon after he was born, but I thanked God all the more that He'd given me this wonderful baby boy. Then when my boy was five years old, he got sick. The doctor told me it was serious and told me to be strong, because he was not sure he could save my boy or not. He was preparing me for the worst and I felt like my whole world would collapse if I lost my son. He was all I had, and I loved him so."

Norman listened as the waitress continued her story: "Then a neighbor gave me one of your sermons to read. In it you said, 'If you have a loved one who is ill or about whom you are worried, don't hold this loved one too closely. Surrender him to God. God gave him to you. He isn't yours, really, he is God's. So give him to God, for God is good. He's a great, kind, loving Father who holds each of His children in His love."

She started to get emotional, but Norman asked her to keep going. "Well, I'd never heard anything like that before. And it seemed awfully hard to do, but something inside me told me it was right. So I prayed the way you said, and put my boy in God's keeping." And she held out her hands as if she were lifting up a child into the great arms of God.

"And what happened?" Norman gently asked.

Smiling through tears of joy, she said, "Isn't God good? He let me keep my son. And now God and I are raising him together." A number of other waitresses had joined them by now and stood listening. There were tears in everybody's eyes, including my husband's. I was emotional, too, when I heard that, knowing that my work on Norman's sermons had made a difference. I guess there are often tears when you come into the presence of that kind of happiness.

Several years ago when an editor at *Guideposts* wrote a short devotional about how she had once knitted sweaters for a relief organization to distribute to needy children, several readers wrote in wanting to know more. Then our editors decided to run an article in the magazine on the subject and we were shocked at the response: Over twenty thousand readers wrote to ask us for a pattern so they could knit sweaters too! We had barely mentioned the need, but to this day we've received over ninety thousand sweaters for children in countries such as Turkey, India and Mozambique. I believe it happened because people wanted to give of themselves.

So you see, service can take on a variety of forms. Whether it's knitting sweaters or sitting on a committee, we can give a part of ourselves and feel a great joy in the process. But service does not have to stop there. Often words of encouragement and appreciation can serve a person well, especially on days when they really need them. One family we know has made a habit of appreciation with a sort of dinner-table game that they've worked out over the years.

One particular night, though, the father came home from an unusually difficult day at work and when he sat down to dinner with his family, he commented:

"This day has been a little dreary for me, I'll admit it. But there must be some good things about it. Let's each try to name one good thing about today."

So around the table they went. One of the children thought that the rain would make the farmers happy. Another said she liked the sound the raindrops made on the roof. A third said gravely that the day must be a good day because God had made it the way it was. The father smiled and said that it was a good day because they had good friends visiting them.

Then it was the mother's turn, "It's a good day," she said, "because we're all together." She gazed at her husband. "But the best thing about this day, or any day," she said to him, "is you."

Appreciation is certainly one of the best of all methods to serve others and to light a glow in somebody's heart. When you show appreciation, you will also feel the warmth of it in your own heart.

My oldest daughter experienced this kind of appreciation last summer when she and her husband Paul moved from Pittsburgh to Pawling. They decided they could move here on their own without hiring movers, and so they packed and packed for days before they were supposed to drive across Pennsylvania and into New York. But suddenly, they realized they weren't going to make it in time. Not only had the load been greater than they expected, but Paul was struggling with his health. They felt, however, that God would provide.

Then a friend knocked on their door one sunny afternoon and *told* them (she didn't ask!) that they needed help. The day after that she came back and packed up all their books. The very next day another person from their home Bible study group came over and told Maggie she was going to clean out the shelves in the basement. She had noticed that Maggie—who, like many of us, has had trouble asking for help—seemed frazzled when she saw her the week before, and figured she probably needed an extra pair of hands. That friend stayed all day working in the basement.

When they were actually ready to move, another friend had come and asked what he could do. Well, by that time, Maggie was willing to let people help by cleaning out the pantry, or the medicine closet, or whatever else needed done. These friends really served my daughter, and it was a blessing to hear their story. In return, as she and Paul were driving out of town she ran into another friend whom she knew never had two cents to her name. Maggie had a gift certificate to a local grocery store that she knew she couldn't use, so she stopped the car and handed the certificate to the grateful woman.

The great thing about service, you see, is that the more you experience it—either by giving or receiving—the more you want to serve. I like how the Apostle Paul described it in II Corinthians 9:6, "He who sows sparingly will also reap sparingly, and he who sows bountifully will also reap bountifully." We ought to be extravagantly generous in helping meet the needs of other people.

One way I have seen this extravagant service is through the service of prayer. As a result of Norman's books, our Guideposts magazines, or our ongoing work at the Peale Center, we receive thousands of requests for prayer from people all over the world. And regularly, our staff stops in the middle of a working day, to pray together for these requests. I believe praying for others is one of the greatest gifts we can give them. We started twenty-five years ago by simply offering a day of prayer every season. But we've realized this has not only helped the people we are trying to serve, it has changed our lives as well. Consequently, prayer has become a hallmark of our organization. It's even changed the place where we live. When we first started publishing from Pawling, the local post office was quite small. Now, with the volume of mail they receive for the Peale Center, the U.S. Postal service has had to upgrade the post office to a first class place!

A few months ago, I returned from a speaking engagement in Alabama. I expected about fifty women at this luncheon, but imagine my surprise when over three hundred were waiting for me when I walked into the room. (I guess they didn't really believe that a ninety-four-year-old woman would travel five states away to talk with them!) I shared with them some of my experiences as a pastor's wife, what it meant to be available to others and the need most of us feel to find someone we can talk with. Then I challenged them, asking whether there was a strategy in place at their churches to help meet the needs of others and solve their problems. It was a simple as that.

You can take this concept of service and expand it into the new century because we're now more aware of a larger world out there, not just a community or city or even a country. We live in a world where it doesn't make any difference if you're in America or India or Switzerland. We're seeing more of a world culture coming together; we can see on the evening news help given to those in need because of an earthquake or a flood or some other natural disaster. We are more aware of world problems than ever before and I believe that means we can help people more. It is as if we're more directly inter-related. And this provides us with a great opportunity that we must seize, and act upon.

As we take steps to incorporate positive thinking into successful Christian living, I'm convinced we need to make a service-investment with our finances. The Bible calls this tithing, which is a little like casting bread upon the waters that returns many-fold. I don't think we can logically explain why this principle is true. But from experience I have learned that it is. The Bible tells us, "Bring ye all tithes into the storehouses . . ." (Malachi 3:10). I remember what Norman said once: "I would be afraid not to tithe, because it might stop the flow of God's abundance." We really believed that throughout our lives, and I still believe it now.

But I also think investing your time is another way of saying, "I'm going to think of others besides myself." If you're not careful as you grow older, your own needs, ambitions, and dreams will overshadow your thinking of other people. We want to guard against that as much as we possibly can. So I recommend tithing our time.

Some churches do a better job of that than others. I remember visiting one large church where they had a huge warehouse with volunteers distributing food to the needy. In one area were canned goods; in another was a bakery. We stopped at the butcher shop and the guide who was taking us around said, "I want you to look in that butcher shop. There are three men there.

Can you pick out the one who is paid as a full time staff member, and which two are volunteers?" Well, of course, we couldn't. But that was a good demonstration of what he was trying to show us: that everyone can serve.

Not long ago I was on a bus in New York City. It stopped to pick up a large, red-faced woman who seemed very angry about something. Evidently, she put the wrong amount of money in the coin box, because the driver had to call her back and ask for more. This seemed to infuriate her, and she shouted a loud refusal. When he persisted, courteously enough, she flung another coin into the box.

But then she demanded his badge number. He was rude, she said, and she would report him to the authorities. After she took his number and tramped to the rear of the bus, the episode seemed over. But a small voice seemed to whisper in my ear, "You can do something." So I went up to the driver and said, "I, too, would like your number. I want to report to your superiors that you have been calm and courteous under trying circumstances not your fault." He gave me a quick smile and his number.

I wrote that letter and had a prompt reply thanking me and saying my commendation would go into the driver's file. A small happening, to be sure. But you know, I got a tremendous lift out of it. Why? Because in a tiny way, I had tried to balance the great scales of justice that tremble in front of all of us all the time.

Service is not a very difficult gift to offer others; we all qualify to serve, for when we find a need, our job is simply to fill it. And as we do, we have discovered the secret of true joy!

⇜ TAKE IT WITH YOU! ⇝

"How many outlets for serving others do you have in your life right now? Remember, if you double them, you will quadruple your chances for obtaining this thing called happiness!"

7

This Planet Called Relationships

Be devoted to one another in brotherly love.
Honor one another above yourselves.

—Romans 12:10 (NIV)

ATELY, I HAVE BEEN NOTICING a troubling trend: People are lonely. It seems every time I travel to speak somewhere, or read a letter at the Peale Center for Christian Living, I hear about the painful circumstances of someone's lonely life. Whether it's a breakdown in communication between husband and wife, or a person who does not know how to make friends, or an estranged son who feels he can never go back to his parents, many individuals in this new millennium are struggling with feelings of loneliness. As life has become faster and busier, I think it's also gotten lonelier for many people. If we're honest with ourselves, not many of us can get through this world without feeling loneliness at some time or another. We all long for relationships that will give us meaning and make us happy.

But that is no easy thing, as we also know. Without the proper people skills and personal beliefs, it is often difficult to enter this sometimes strange territory called relationships. As one young women recently said to me, she thought relationships were a little like going to another planet! Most of the time, you wonder where the other person is coming from and if you have anything at all in common. So you put on your protective gear, and brace yourself for the ride. Yet there is something strangely inviting about the companionship and so you are willing at least to explore this other galaxy. (And certainly, there are some relationships that make us feel like we *are* entering another orbit altogether.)

Then there are those people who have a nice habit of bringing us back to earth and helping us breathe a little more easily and normally again. Whether we like it or not, this strange planet called relationships is as essential to our well being and growth as breathing; we just need to know a few cosmic principles to achieve successful and meaningful interactions with other human creatures!

To begin with, I think it might be helpful to examine the current age we live in, an age where it seems more and more people are searching for significant relationships than they did even fifty years ago. For instance, when Norman and I were becoming friends, there were no such things as personal ads placed in the local newspaper or on the Internet to pursue a relationship. Though my grandchildren can hardly believe it when I tell them, there was, a time when there were no computers, let alone the Internet, either! Today, however, we have more information available to us through technology than ever before in the history of the world, more opportunities to live longer through medical advancements, and more products to choose from for daily living than at any other time. A recent news article even said e-mail has far eclipsed hand-delivered letters in sheer volume, and there are signs that it's pushing other kinds of communication out of the way as well.

I wonder, though, if all these signs of progress have made it more challenging for people simply to interact with one another. The result, of course, is increased loneliness. Just last month I read about a study done at the University of Chicago that concluded loneliness undermines a person's physical health by altering his cardiac functions and disrupting his sleep. Apparently, doctors have known for some time that lonely people do not live as long and have more medical problems than non-lonely people. The new research demon-strates that lonely people perceive the world as threat-ening, and so their orientation to others *reduces* positive feedback or emotional support. These per-spectives can ultimately lead to higher blood pressure and sleep disruptions, factors that have in turn been shown to have an impact on the body's resilience in dealing with disease. Our personal health should be one reason alone that we develop some helpful strate-gies for landing on this planet called relationships!

Obviously, people need to be in relationships, but today they are finding it more and more difficult. Walk into any bookstore and you'll know that people are starving to find out what works for them in building relationships. Self-help books that enhance every aspect of a person's life are on best-seller lists everywhere. The only problem is they have often forgotten to include the great relationship builder of the cosmos, God.

When Norman first published his book, *The Power of Positive Thinking,* some people criticized it as a self-help book instead of a theological book. This confused my dear husband greatly, because he always believed it was not a self-help book; rather, it was what he liked to call a "God-help" book. Throughout its pages, Norman described several Christian principles to encourage people to have stronger, more meaningful relationships in their families, their jobs and their communities. In fact, at the core of Norman's belief (and mine, too) was that "we can do all things through Christ who gives us strength," and that "nothing is impossible with God."

I have already noted that I believe we need to start with our relationship with God as we approach anything in life, especially something so dear as our relationships with other people. He has given us plenty of sound advice in the Bible for loving one another, but He has also set an example for us in how His Son Jesus

Christ interacted with others. So as we turn the eyes of our hearts toward growing in our relationship with our Heavenly Father, I believe our relationships with other humans on earth will become easier and more natural. Besides, we have no idea what God might have planned in using us with others.

I still remember, for instance, the time in the early 1970s when Norman and I went to the home of some friends in New York City for dinner. After the meal, we saw a household item that interested us and we asked where they got it. They told us of a little store in Manhattan where we could pick up something like it. "And by the way," they said, "when you go there, ask for Mr. Benton. He's the young man who sold us this. He was very obliging and helpful."

A day or two later during our lunch hour at the church office, Norman and I stopped by the store and asked for Mr. Benton. We were told he was out to lunch, but could anyone else help us?

Ordinarily, we would have said yes. But for some reason, Norman responded by telling the salesperson that we'd come back later. As we left the store, I asked him why we didn't just look now. I wondered what difference it made who sold it to us.

But Norman believed we should wait, that Mr. Benton had been recommended to us and he wondered if there might not be a small commission in it for him. "Besides," he said as we walked on the busy New York sidewalk, "I feel I should see *him* for some reason."

So late in the afternoon, my husband and I went back to the little shop. Only this time, Mr. Benton had gone down to a warehouse to see about a shipment that had just come in. Could anyone else be of service? Again, Norman shook his head, and decided we'd wait and come back later. I grew irritated and told him he could come back but I had too much to do to keep running in and out of this store looking for Mr. Benton!

Two days later Norman went back to the store. This time he found Mr. Benton in his office, a handsome young man but seemingly discontent. A painful loneliness filled his eyes. Norman introduced himself and told him that some friends had sent him to see if Mr. Benton could help in buying a certain item.

The young man's face grew softer. "I know who you are, Dr. Peale, but your friends didn't send you here," he said to Norman.

Norman was taken aback. "They didn't?"

"No," said Mr. Benton, "God sent you. I've been terribly lonely, and on the verge of killing myself because I don't deserve to live. I planned to do it last weekend. Then I decided to wait one more week—this week—

and ask God one more time to send me help. And here you are."

When he heard that, Norman got up, walked over to the office door and closed it. "Tell me about it," he said to the young man.

Mr. Benton poured out a tragic story about his involvement with his best friend's wife. The friend was in Vietnam, and the woman had become pregnant. Overwhelmed with guilt and remorse, she had committed suicide. Now her lover felt that he should impose the same punishment on himself. It was one of those devastating situations that ministers are often called to face.

How glad I was that Norman had paid attention to his personal relationship with God to seek out this young man and offer him help. Was it just coincidence? Mr. Benton didn't think so. I didn't either. A soul in torment had cried out to God for help, and God answered (as He so often does) by sending another living human being.

Calling on all his pastoral experience, all his understanding of fallible human beings, all his spiritual insight, Norman was able to offer a measure of peace to the troubled young man and eventually helped him start rebuilding his shattered life. He pointed him to Jesus and invited him to church.

That's the starting point to positive relationships with others: asking God for help. With that as our anchor, I believe there are then a number of other ways we can ensure strong and substantial relationships with others. Whether it's a marriage, a friendship, or a "chance" introduction or acquaintance, these specific attributes help us navigate our way through the some-times challenging planet of relationships.

At the beginning of this chapter, you may have noticed that I listed a Bible verse from Romans, chapter 12: "Be devoted to one another with brotherly love." Devotion—or commitment—to other individu-als is one of the greatest gifts you can offer someone. No marriage can last without it, no employer will appreciate his employee apart from it, and no true friendship can be sustained unless there's an ongoing commitment. Conflict certainly will arise in any rela-tionship we encounter, but we should resist what might be our natural inclination to run from it, and stay com-mitted to the betterment of the other. Even though some people suggest we live in a disposable society these days where difficult, messy things easily get thrown away—including relationships—I believe we'll experience great joy if we're willing to stay committed to others.

Next, I have always found acceptance to be an essential ingredient in the making of strong relationships. If love and devotion are to last, there must be acceptance of the sometimes difficult truth that all of us have faults and failings, and that we're not going to change the basic personality of someone until he or she wants to change.

Many times this happens *only* through one of the most powerful, yet difficult elements, of any relationship: forgiveness. We *must* learn to forgive people, for like loneliness, unforgiveness and resentment not only do terrible damage to a person's emotional well-being, but his physical health deteriorates as well.

Once my administrative assistant handed me a letter, and as I started to read it, I was struck again by how essential forgiveness is. It began, "I have a serious problem and I need help. I have a very bad grudge against someone I used to think so much of. I have built up a terrible amount of resentment against this person to the point that I cannot sleep at night and have become depressed."

As I read these words, I thought to myself, how sad that the act of forgiveness is so difficult for so many people. That letter echoed the same problem I see repeatedly in relationships: a wife can't forgive her husband's infidelity; a daughter cannot forgive her mother's verbal abuse; an employee cannot forgive his boss's criticism; a friend cannot forgive another for feeling betrayed. The list goes on and on.

But equally important is our inability to forgive ourselves for past transgressions. When we cannot move on from our mistakes, we live in a dark cloud that keeps us from enjoying other people in authentic relationships. Ultimately, this failure on our part really will make us ill—mentally, spiritually, and physically.

Right now is the time to re-examine seriously those people whom we consider unforgivable, so that we can begin the healing process in our relationships. Here's what's helped me through the years whenever I found it difficult to let go of a grudge. First, simply determine to forgive. The Apostle Paul wrote, "Let all bitterness, wrath, anger clamor and evil speaking be put away from you, with all malice. And be kind to one another, tenderhearted, forgiving one another, just as God in Christ also has forgiven you" (Ephesians 4:31-32). This simple, direct blueprint should become our mantra as we set our minds to the act of forgiveness.

The act of feeling sincere forgiveness toward another is not easy. The longer you hold onto a resentment, the harder it is to eradicate that ugly feeling. Sooner or later, you'll watch the resentment become a habit. To break away, you have to decide that, no matter what, you will be forgiving toward anyone who has hurt you.

As part of your determination, you then need to take concrete steps. It might help to make a list of those people you need to forgive. If you need to forgive yourself, include your own name. Then, beside each name, write down how you've been hurt by that person. Next, set a date and time for the acts of forgiveness to take place, but be realistic. Don't expect to perform a blanket act of forgiveness by tomorrow noon! Take seriously the idea that you are going to work conscientiously to forgive each person on your list. Each of these actions may take some time. Finally, beside each name, write down a way for you to communicate your forgiveness to the person involved. You may consider writing a letter, making a phone call or paying a visit. Whatever you choose, bring God into the process by seeking His wisdom as you write, phone or visit. He'll guide your words if you turn to Him for help.

As a minister's wife for over fifty years in the same church in the same city, I often felt that I had to be careful about how I spent time with different people in our congregation. Although I was secure in my own purpose, I felt it might be better to keep to myself in most cases so as not to run the risk of offending anyone. I learned a long time before that some people like "knowing" the minister's family (or community leaders) because it somehow makes them feel important about themselves. But it also gives them a chance to gossip if they want to, so I was extremely cautious about my close relationships. It probably helped that I have always tended to be a private person by nature anyway. It also helped that I was terribly busy serving on many different organizational committees as well as raising a family. I honestly didn't have much time for outside relationships, but this proved to be the best method for me in relating to individuals at our church.

It was not easy, though. Sometimes, people misunderstood me or my intentions and said things that made me feel very bad. And sometimes people in the religious community criticized Norman for his simple explanations of Christian faith. Not only that, but staying in the same church for so long while people came and went—New York City is an extremely transient place—was emotionally challenging. Whenever these things bothered me, I had to learn, with God's help, to go through these steps of forgiveness. I knew that the longer I waited to forgive, the worse my attitude would get about everything. So now, after ninety-four years of living, I have learned it's best to try to accept others—no matter what they say or do—and forgive them quickly if I have felt hurt by them.

My daughter Maggie told me just last week of a recent conversation she had had with a friend of hers whose mother is also in her nineties, and who also found it necessary to be somewhat cautious in making friends. It seems this woman had been involved in politics in the South at a time—and in a place—when women were usually expected to stay at home. She became a public figure throughout the Deep South and so she, too, felt she had to guard her time with others, not wanting anyone to feel unnecessarily overlooked or disrespected. Of course, as I had, she had many professional relationships with others in her work, relationships that were stimulating and rewarding and fulfilling. Still, she knew friendships were sensitive business and sometimes difficult to nurture.

Today's times are probably a little different in these regards. I know many ministers and their spouses who have been able to cultivate significant friendships with members of their congregations without offending others. But they agree that we all need to exercise wisdom and integrity as we foster relationships, devoting ourselves to them as God leads, and accepting one another through a constant attitude of forgiveness.

Small, thoughtful acts of consideration also help keep relationships grounded in the reality of planet earth. It's no secret that we all have needs, insecurities, fears and hopes, and that most of us thrive when we are encouraged or affirmed to pursue our gifts or dreams. When you think about it, we really become our best when those closest to us consider our feelings by consistently expressing their concern and placing our welfare ahead of theirs. This becomes a comfort and a strength for us in difficult times. It also makes each day a little easier.

Norman always loved to encourage other people. Every time we traveled somewhere together, I always had to hurry him along because he liked chatting with the cab drivers, or the hotel clerks, or whomever happened to step into his path. But he also had a way of making even corporate presidents or governmental leaders feel encouraged. On the same day that we'd be visiting the president of the United States and his family at the White House, for instance, Norman could engage in a wonderful conversation with the driver of the car sent to pick us up. It didn't matter who he talked with throughout his long life (and he talked with *a lot* of leaders, bankers, ministers, presidents, actors, generals, teachers, drivers—you name it), he always tried to affirm their individuality and enjoy their personality. Maybe it was his genuine humility or his sincere desire to learn from others that kept doors opening for Norman. Mostly, I think it was that he truly believed every single person he encountered had a unique story and therefore something to learn from.

And I, too, have found that to be true.

Such a positive approach to relationships is a perspective that can be developed over time. One way to do that is, ironically, by spending time alone. We all need to be alone once in a while, for it is while we're alone that we can work on ourselves. Even Jesus needed solitude on more than one occasion. And He always seemed to seek it out when He needed to pray or work through a problem.

Making the most of our time alone helps us to become more interesting both to ourselves and to others. During these quiet personal times, we can draw closer in our relationship to God, we can do some soul-searching, or we can read a book that enriches our lives. The point is, we can help our personalities flourish.

Norman and I often advised people suffering from loneliness to try hard to keep their personalities alive. "You do not want to let the lamp go out," I remember him saying to others. Then he'd always ask this question: "How can you expect to make an impression, to captivate and stimulate, unless you keep that personality spark alive?"

So if you're lonely, you should also do a self-examination of your personality. Is there something about the way you behave that repels or invites people? Do you act kindly toward others, or do you easily lose your patience? Are you quick to criticize or to encourage? Such was the case of one woman who once consulted my husband for some relationship advice. It seemed this woman, Betty, didn't have a friend in the world. She would go home after a long day at work, cook herself dinner, watch television or read the newspaper, and then go to bed. Every night she repeated this routine, and every morning her loneliness grew. She vigorously insisted to Norman that the real cause of loneliness was her difficulty making friends in such a large city as New York.

When Norman delved a little deeper into her personality, he found that she was highly critical of everyone she knew. He also found out that her past roommate had terminated their living arrangement when Betty didn't do her share of the housework or meet her share of the expenses.

The more Norman looked into this woman's childhood, the more problems he found. Then he helped her to understand why she was so hypercritical of others. Slowly, her attitudes changed, and slowly, she became involved in her local church. Then she joined a drama club. Her new interests led to new acquaintances, and eventually, to new friends. All of this was brought about when she learned that her loneliness was the result of her personal attitudes toward others.

So it might be important for you to reflect on how you come across to others. Do you project a friendly, affirming air? If not, act as if you are friendly. I'm a firm believer in the "as-if" principle we often suggested to others: If you continuously act a certain way, this behavior becomes reality. Acting friendly is simply showing an interest in another person. It doesn't take much to greet someone warmly and take the time to listen to what he has to say.

It might also be helpful to have a plan for each day. When you're lonely and think you have nothing to look forward to, your loneliness is going to seem amplified. The antidote is to have a flexible plan for each new day.

Each morning, after I finish my two-mile walk, I still like to make a list of things to do. I always include activities that will put me in contact with at least two other people, even if the contact is over the phone. I also try to encourage others to plan as often as possible outings to inexpensive public places you enjoy, a favorite park, a museum or the library. It's easy to check the newspaper for free concerts, plays, meetings of groups or clubs that might interest you. Of course, a local church always has activities to be a part of. Or if you're an avid bridge player, or love to paint, it is not difficult to find out if there's a local bridge club or an art class to enroll in. In other words, if you pursue a particular interest, you'll meet other people who share this same interest. And I have always found that it's much easier to make new friends when you already have a common bond.

Because I have been working outside of my home all these years, I, like many women, have lost contact with friends I had years ago. Since it's not always easy being sociable when you come home tired from a job, I tried to set a goal to invite a friend or loved one to lunch at least once a week. Perhaps you could do the same. If you're blessed by knowing several people whose company you relish, set up a standing engagement to meet with each individual on specific days every month. This way, you can also give yourself something to look forward to each day.

Basically, this planet called relationships has different meanings to different people, just as there are different layers of friendships. Some last a few years, and some are much more intimate than others. I personally found that many fulfilling relationships grew either from our family or out of our work as ministers. I have a lot of good relationships with people who are important to me, but I don't necessarily see them often or grow with them personally. Sometimes in life we need simply the support of another human presence to keep our lives interesting or stimulating. But as the old saying goes, the best way to make a friend is to be one!

I have been enriched many times over by people I never became close friends with, people who still probably have no idea how they contributed to my life and growth. Whether it was through women in committees or in the Red Cross that met regularly at our church, board members of the American Bible Society or our denomination, or the wives of governmental leaders or other religious figures, I have always found myself in the company of fascinating people. And that in turn has made my life all the more interesting.

Whenever I was with Norman and he would stop to talk with someone, I always benefited from his genuine interest in other people. He had a reporter's instinct as well as a caring instinct. He knew what questions to ask people to help elicit the responses, and he was naturally engaged in their lives. I probably learned more from my husband about relationships than I did from anyone else, specifically that this is a good way to stop thinking about yourself and start thinking of others.

Back in the summer of 1943 (some of you who are reading this probably feel that is ancient history!), we were invited by our friend Lowell Thomas to visit his estate in upstate New York. We enjoyed the little town, especially because it was so accessible to New York, yet far enough away to be in the real country. While taking a much needed break there, we heard of a small farm for sale on a hill not far from Lowell's place. We decided to go look. What could it hurt to look?

Since Norman and I married in 1930, we had never owned a home of our own, an actual place where the children could put down roots. (We rented a few different apartments at different times in New York City.) Well, I was immediately enchanted by the eighteenth-century farmhouse, the great maples, and the view across the valley. Norman wasn't so sure; he felt the house was too big for us. Besides, he knew the place with its twenty acres cost twenty-five thousand dollars (I laugh at the price now!) and we didn't even have five thousand dollars.

I suggested we borrow the initial finances, but my husband had an aversion to debt. When I reminded him that he could go out and give lectures to pay it back, he frowned at me. But eventually he relented because he knew this quiet old farmhouse could meet both our family and our spiritual needs. The following January we moved in, though we kept our apartment in the city, of course, and were able to travel easily back and forth between urban and country living. At that point, Norman was delighted! He even named it Sugar

Tree Farm in memory of Sugar Tree Ridge, the little Ohio village where Norman's father, Clifford, had first taken his bride a half century before.

I grew vegetables each summer and canned them for the winter. Norman used the time there to reflect and write. We took long walks through meadows together and chatted in town with new neighbors. The children played and explored the countryside on the weekends, and enjoyed the benefits of city life during the week. It was the best of both worlds.

Why do I tell you this story now? Because when our family moved to that old house on Quaker Hill outside of Pawling, New York, we found a wonderful community of people with whom we have been very fortunate to establish solid friendships. Many city and state leaders had already purchased summer homes there, so it has been nice to be among so many interesting people. After we retired, we moved here year round and continued worshiping at Christ Church on Quaker Hill, another supportive community of Christian friends. This is the place where our children grew up, and now their children are playing there, too. It's been a geographical anchor for our relationships.

It's also the place where ideas percolated and very often found life through the encouragement of other friends. One such idea grew out of conversations we had had our friend Raymond Thornburg. Raymond was a Pawling businessman who supported the Christian work we did. Perhaps that is why he made the suggestion one day that we ought to consider publishing more of Norman's sermons. He observed how in the business world there were many weekly or monthly newsletters purporting to give subscribers inside information on industrial trends or forthcoming legislation. Why not, he asked us, put out a sort of spiritual newsletter for businessmen or factory workers or ordinary families with simple down-to-earth stories of religious faith in action?

We talked some more. Such a periodical, we decided, might help to break down some of the barriers that still existed between the church and the business world. It could remind people that our personal freedoms were gifts from God, and it could be nonsectarian with the intention of harmonizing religious diversities and reducing friction among Catholic, Protestant and Jew. It could utilize the old proven testimonial technique, encouraging ordinary, everyday people who had found a firm faith to stand up and be counted. Celebrities might be persuaded to tell how, through the application of religion, they had learned to live victoriously in their relationships and vocations. Finally, it would serve as a medium for bringing to people our faith in Christianity as a practical method for solving life's problems.

Of course, not all of our friends and acquaintances were initially enthusiastic about the idea. Wouldn't the material have a deadly monotony, they'd ask. Wouldn't people be reluctant to discuss anything as personal as the part religion played in their lives? Besides, if there was no advertising, where would the operating expenses come from?

At first, none of us had any answers. But slowly God began to provide in the ways he always provides: through other people. Finances, ideas and talent came to us through new and old friends, and together, we published the first issue of *Guideposts* magazine. When it almost folded after the second year, friends again encouraged us to keep going, to pray that subscribers would be faithful in supporting the magazine. They were. Eventually, it grew so much that we needed to buy new land in Pawling and build a bigger place to run the magazine and ministry! Before long, the circulation of *Guideposts* expanded into the largest of any religious-based magazine in the country, an honor it still holds to this day at the turn of a new century. And all because a few friends got together, dreamed big and then passed that dream on through real, human stories about faith and relationships—subjects that never grow old.

I don't think Norman and I could ever have imagined that our marriage, which spanned six decades, could have been so full of such wonderful people, people who always encouraged us as we tried to encourage others. But that's what life is really about: building meaningful relationships that sometimes are out of this world!

⚜ TAKE IT WITH YOU! ⚜

"Reflect in a moment of solitude on how you might come across to others. Ask God to help you be a better friend and then look for opportunities to reach out!"

8

Work of the
Heart

Whatever you do, work at it with all your heart, as working for the Lord, not for men.

—COLOSSIANS 3:23 (NIV)

THE FIRST TIME I realized I had a hearing problem was over thirty years ago. I was trying to listen to my watch tick one day and found I couldn't hear a thing. With my left ear I could still hear the ticking, but not with my right. I was barely sixty years old at the time, so I certainly was not expecting to lose my hearing at so young an age. But when I consulted a doctor, he confirmed my concern, though he was not sure why my right ear was going deaf.

Months of testing and examinations followed. Fortunately, the hearing in my left ear remained normal. If a person sat on my "deaf" side, though, I had to twist my head awkwardly to hear. It was frustrating, to say the least, especially given our busy schedule traveling and speaking.

Eventually, my doctors came to the conclusion that my problem was otosclerosis, an overgrowth on a tiny bone called the stapes inside my right ear. This bone is the smallest in the human body; ten of them would just about cover your smallest fingernail. It's shaped like a stirrup and is the closest bone to the auditory nerve. Sound makes the stapes vibrate. This stimulates the nerve, which in turn sends the sound-message to the brain where its meaning is deciphered. But in my case the stapes had become rigid, unable to vibrate or react to sound.

Time went by. More treatments and one operation didn't seem to help. Then our family physician told me of a New York surgeon who had developed a new technique for such ear problems. Apparently, it was a real breakthrough, so of course I was anxious to meet this remarkable man.

Dr. Samuel Rosen was in his early seventies when I first met him, and I immediately felt comfortable with him. He was gentle, reassuring and fatherly. When I told him about my problem and asked if he could help me, he smiled. "If God is willing," he said.

He used the same phrase during subsequent visits when I came in for testing. One day I asked him why and Dr. Rosen gave me an answer that I have never forgotten: "When my parents prayed," he said, "whether it was a prayer of supplication or of thanks, they always ended it with, 'If God is willing.' That's a cornerstone of my faith and work."

The kind doctor went on to tell me a bit of his story and how he developed his unique work ethic. His parents were immigrants who struggled to make ends meet when they first arrived in the United States. His father peddled crockery and his mother suffered from severe asthma. One morning, when he was six years old and preparing to go to school, young Samuel's mother had such a severe attack that she could not catch her breath. To a child, that meant she would suffocate, but even when a doctor came and gave her some medicine that relieved her, the young boy was still not so easily convinced. He sat by her bedside all day. Then he told his mother that someday he would be a doctor so he could cure her. When she heard that, his mother took Samuel's hand in hers and said, "If God is willing."

God was willing. Samuel Rosen's brothers pooled their savings and sent him to medical school. For over forty years he was an ear surgeon at Mt. Sinai Hospital in New York City and taught surgery in its medical school. And it was Dr. Rosen who discovered in 1952 what needed to be done to combat otosclerosis. For eighteen intense months, every evening after his day's work was done, he researched the stapes of the ear and designed three dozen special instruments that could help restore a patient's hearing.

When Dr. Rosen discovered at last the delicate instrument that would go on to open the ears of thousands of people—including me—he finally understood what his mother had meant those early years: God was willing! He knew he could not have persevered in such important work without God's help. He then went on to publish his findings in medical journals, demonstrate and teach his new procedure in forty-five countries, and train (at no charge) thousands of doctors to perform the same operation he performed on me. They in turn taught others, and as a result of his heart-felt work, millions of partially deaf people now hear fully.

If ever there was a clear example of what our values for work should be, Dr. Rosen is it. His desire to become a doctor grew out of a deeply personal experience with his mother. Then he gave one hundred percent of his efforts to his studies and continued the same determined attitude while researching and practicing his medicine. Even when he was discouraged, he did not give up nor did he go looking for a new career. Ultimately, he put each patient, each study, each operation in God's hands, knowing that He was the one who could bring about success.

Now almost fifty years later, when so many people are either consumed by their careers or miserable in them, Dr. Rosen's example provides some refreshing lessons. I know that today many people will do whatever they need to just to get ahead, even if that means stepping on people along the way. It seems our competitive, often cutthroat market has made it more difficult for people to honestly work at their jobs with all their heart. Instead, I've encountered many troubling stories of how a person's employment has made him more likely to develop emotional stress or health problems, miss out on quality times with his family and never really get ahead financially. Maybe these negative consequences are because our priorities have become mixed up and workers—from CEOs to the low person on the ladder—often forget to bring their hearts into the marketplace. Even though I'm thankful that our economy is strong, unemployment is low and our society is more high-tech than ever, I believe there are still some old-fashioned ideas that should never leave the workplace. They help maintain a sense of dignity and enjoyment in the one activity that takes more of our time on earth than anything else: our work.

I have been fortunate in my life to be surrounded by people who love their work. Norman was one of the greatest optimists I knew and his positive faith carried over into all he did. Whether it was writing a book or a sermon, or giving a motivational speech to workers at a factory or to businessmen at a sales conference, Norman dove into his work with an enthusiasm that was difficult to match. At the same time, it was contagious, probably because he sincerely derived great joy from his vocation. Consequently, he was always encouraging someone else to "work heartily for the Lord!"

That was important to me, because I, too, wanted to enjoy the work God gave me to do. And after sixty years on dozens of organizational boards and committees, I can honestly tell you that I've loved my work. I suppose it really started for me, though, when I was fourteen years old and I landed my first job as a sales person in a local department store in Detroit. Though you'll have trouble believing it today, I only made eleven dollars a week! But that was fine with me—I was happy to be earning an income in a job I had found on my own, a job that taught me how to get along with people. I wanted to make a little spending money and also help out at home. My father worked hard and gave generously his whole life, but I doubt if he ever earned more than two thousand four hundred dollars a year in his life. My mother had a marked musical gift and played the piano. Sometimes she gave music lessons that also brought in a little extra cash, and both of my brothers always had paper routes. If one of them was sick, Mother and I would get up at five in the morning and walk the route for him. I didn't necessarily enjoy being a substitute paper carrier (especially if it was raining or snowing!), but delivering the papers was a family responsibility. In other words, we all knew what it meant to work hard in order to support each other.

But it took me a while to understand that I had been born with a unique purpose and gifts. In fact, though I earned a college degree to teach, it wasn't really until Norman asked me to serve on many different church committees that I realized what some of my gifts might be. For him, creativity and interacting with people were gifts; I found it easy helping organize our schedules and administrating the business side of the various ministries we were involved in. Together, we challenged each other to develop our gifts to their fullest potential, knowing that this ultimately was what pleased the Lord.

Like Dr. Rosen, Norman never minded working long and hard on his gifts, because he was always wondering if there was something else he could be doing to help the work. For instance, I often remember him finishing one project and then saying, "Now, the next speech I make has got to be good. I have to communicate. Maybe there are people out there who need what I could say, so I've got to be sure that I'm going to do my best." Norman rarely allowed himself to relax in his feeling of responsibility for the work he'd been given to do. Though he was a fun man with a great sense of humor, he took his work very seriously. He had a high standard that he wanted to meet every week, and worked with all his heart at achieving his goals. That is why he left us with an enormous bank of good works and good words, created a week at a time as he developed his gifts.

Perhaps that is why Norman and I always found that one of the saddest things in life was meeting a person with an obvious gift—say, for management or for writing—but who was too afraid to use it. For some reason, he or she always had an excuse, and never dared to try anything new, finding it safer and easier to stay in a job that paid the bills even if it was a job that offered little meaning or inspiration. Why did we always find this so sad? Because when that person chose *not* to pursue his talents, God's special gift in that person remained hidden from the rest of us. Unless we are at least willing to try our hand at something we've always wanted to, we will never truly know what we have to offer others. As Elbert Hubbard said, "The greatest mistake anyone can make is to be afraid of making one."

Can you imagine, for example, a world without Rembrandt or Shakespeare or Benjamin Franklin? If they had ignored their gifts, too afraid to try or of making a mistake, where would we be today? In other words, the gifts God has imparted to each of us need to be developed and put to good use in our work. Just as I benefited greatly because of Dr. Rosen's daring determination to use his gifts as an ear specialist, everyone benefits when we decide to pursue our individual and unique gifts for others.

Several years ago, we had a friend named Charles Ulrich Bay, a very wealthy oilman and ship owner who, at one time, was also the American ambassador to Norway. He also owned the financial firm Kidder, Peabody and Co. His wife Josephine was a clear-minded, intelligent woman—and her tycoon husband recognized her intellectual abilities and used her constantly as a sounding board. "Here's a business proposition that seems pretty good to me," he'd say to her. "Now I want you to argue against it. Tell me what's wrong with it. Poke holes in it. Convince me that it's no good."

Josephine would protest and complain that she didn't know enough about it. Rick would hand her reports and statistics and challenge her to learn everything she could about the proposal so they could discuss it later. For years this challenging give-and-take went on. Then Rick died suddenly and Norman was asked to conduct the funeral. We rode back from the cemetery in the car with Josephine and asked how she was doing. Of course, she did not try to hide the depth of her grief or the extent of her loss. Instead, she admitted that she did not know how she would live without her husband.

Norman looked at her gently and said, "I think I know what Rick would want you to do. He'd want you to take over his work, take charge of everything yourself. Don't you realize that all these years he's been training you to do that? Nobody knows as much about all his enterprises as you do. If ever a husband taught his wife how to get along without him, he did."

Josephine looked stunned. "Do you really believe that I have what it takes to step into his shoes?"

Norman nodded. "What's more, your husband believed it. He obviously thought you had a knack for it. So why don't you make up your mind to do it—and do it?"

Josephine Bay did make up her mind, and became the first woman president of the financial company her husband had built. In the process, she discovered that she really enjoyed her new responsibilities—I've always believed that desire and satisfaction are good indications that you're using your gifts. Josephine then became president of another exporting business her husband had developed—all at a time in our country (the 1950s) when women were usually not running companies. Eventually, she became, in the opinion of many experts, the greatest businesswoman in the United States up until that time. And it all began during those quiet hours in her own home when she made herself willing to learn from her husband and develop her gifts.

Can you imagine, though, what would have happened to Josephine if she had succumbed to fear? Or what would have happened to her husband's businesses if she had not had the heart to pursue her leadership skills? Yet her willingness to risk and try her hand at something she wasn't initially sure about led to a long and splendid career, one that helped many people. Yes, our attitudes about using our gifts in our work should show such courage, even if it means taking a difficult step.

Once we've discovered what particular gifts we've been given, we especially need to make a commitment to nurturing them to their fullest potential. Too often these days, I've found that if people experience a tough work situation, they think they can just quit and move on to another job, trying to find a better position that might make them happy. I think we've lost a sense of commitment to our jobs. Motivational experts will tell you that tenacity, perseverance and diligence are the most effective ingredients to developing a formula for personal success and satisfaction. And employment agencies will tell you that these are the qualities more employers are looking for in new recruits. So just because something gets difficult is no reason to throw away your efforts.

I know this is true. As I've written, when Norman's

book, *The Power of Positive Thinking*, came out, it was an immediate success. It was on the *New York Times* best seller list for over 186 weeks, which at that time was a record. And thousands of people wrote us to tell us how much it had helped them in their faith and in their work. But not everyone was so enthusiastic about it. One clergyman publicly accused Norman of being an "archconservative, a tool of capitalistic interests, who was turning Christianity into a way to get rich." Soon, a few other ministers joined his attacks and published articles calling into question just about everything my husband ever said or did.

Norman, of course, was quite distressed over the comments, and wanted to quit the ministry. He had simply wanted the book to be plain, traditional and easy-to-understand Christianity, written in simple and direct language. Its purpose, he always said, was to show how our Savior Jesus Christ could help people live better lives, how He would help any needy person, just as He had helped Norman.

Still, Norman knew that the best thing to do about criticism or tough situations was to control his anger, study himself and ask, "Is it valid?" If he could then determine if the criticism was valid, he would work to correct himself. If not, then the best possible procedure was to rise above it and not stoop to recrimination.

Not long after that, Norman's father became ill so we boarded a train to visit him. Norman did not want to burden his father with his personal problems, but he had decided he would resign from his work. He wrote out his resignation letter and put it in his jacket pocket, not intending to show his father.

When he walked into the hospital room, however, Norman's eighty year old father could almost read his troubled thoughts. Apparently, he had heard a few of the criticisms, so he went straight to the point and told his son, "Norman, you have always been true and loyal to Jesus Christ. You believe in and preach Bible truths. You are my son, and your old father, who has known good men and not so good men, says you are a good and loyal minister of Jesus Christ." He was then thoughtful and silent for a long pause.

"Besides, and remember this, the Peales never quit. It would break my heart if any one of my sons quit the work God had gifted him for, afraid to stand up and face any situation." Norman smiled when he heard his gentle-spirited father say this—it was just what he needed to hear. And when he walked out of his father's room that day, he reached into his jacket pocket, pulled out the resignation letter, tore it up and threw it in the trash. It was the last time he saw his father alive, but he gave Norman a final gift; he encouraged him not to quit using his gifts.

No, if we gave up our dreams and gifts every time we faced a difficult situation, we might never accomplish anything at all in this world. Enthusiastic commitment to doing the right thing in our work can protect us even when trials come. Besides, our perspective on working needs to include the realization that work opportunities don't necessarily have to end just because a job does, through a lay off or retirement. Not long ago, for instance, my son-in-law, John Allen, took early retirement from his job as an editor at *Reader's Digest*. He had been with *Time* and with *Reader's Digest* for years working as an editor. The weekend after he retired, I called him on the phone Monday morning and said, "John, you don't have any office to go to. What are you going to do?" He confessed that he wasn't quite sure and knew it would be a strange adjustment to leave a career he loved. Then I got an idea.

"Tell you what. I'll give you a desk, a telephone, half a secretary and no money." I wanted him to come and work at the Peale Center for Christian Living, helping us with decisions about this project or that publication. He took it! Even though he's not on our payroll, we get the benefit of his sound editorial advice, and he continues to work in a field that he enjoys, using gifts he's nurtured over a lifetime in hours that he sets. He has important work to do for us in carrying on Norman's ministry of practical Christianity. In fact, we pass many things by John—from articles to book ideas to marketing tools. He feels that his work has continued and we feel that we've found an essential leader in our ministry. This kind of work ethic allows everyone to win.

In a similar way, our next-door neighbor decided that he would literally give away his insurance company—which was very successful—to his children and enter retirement earlier than he had planned. So I called him, too, and said, "Listen, I'll tell you what I'll do. I'll give you a desk, a telephone, half a secretary and no money." I knew his financial expertise could help us in our work. He took it, too! Every morning now he comes in to review our entire list of wills and analyze them. He's scoured over our planned giving portfolio and our other financial documents to make sure our organization is in proper order. He's offered us a marvelous service that has saved us extra money while he has received the opportunity to keep his hand in a field he loves.

But these two situations did not just happen. They came about because these two talented men had spent a lifetime cultivating strong work habits and developing their professional gifts. They also passed on to their children similar habits and beliefs.

I always try to encourage my own children in their careers, asking them how they're doing, what their goals and challenges and dreams are. For instance, my grandson, Clifford (named for Norman's father) is a business reporter for a Cincinnati newspaper. It's funny how I can even now remember encouraging him to write when he was a little boy; imagine how much I enjoy it when he sends me stories he's written!

Another grandson, Chris, just got a job in Colorado Springs as a sales manager, and since he's required to motivate his team, he's been poring over Norman's books and videos to help him understand how to do so! Hard work isn't just reporting to a place and punching the time clock. It's knowing exactly what you're working for, understanding and acknowledging your goal and learning to do the best you can each day. It's giving your whole heart. That's the understanding we grew up with and that's what we passed on to our children, and what they passed on to their children. Since Norman and I both worked in jobs outside the homes, my children watched us caring for others in a variety of ways. So all three became adults who were involved in the community, were active on boards, and developed their gifts for the benefit of others.

Still, I'd be foolish to suggest that it is as easy as pie to make each and every day as productive as we'd like it to be. It is not. Events and circumstances happen in ways that often catch us by surprise and usually divert our attention from our well planned "to do" list. But over the years, I've found that there are a few things you can do to make your work more fulfilling as well as more consistently productive.

The other morning, my mind raced as I thought of all the things I had to accomplish that day. Even at ninety-four years of age, I'm used to busy days, and most of the time I enjoy them. But this morning, I felt overwhelmed by the responsibilities facing me. As I rushed through the house, getting ready to go to the office, I glanced at a framed photograph of Norman. All of a sudden, I felt less agitated, remembering what a calming influence Norman always had on me. At that moment, I relaxed a little, and walked into the study to pray. I immediately felt my mind clearing, my energy level rising and God's peaceful strength filling me. I was ready to make my day a productive one.

Norman used to tease me about the notes I made for myself, and my need to squeeze as much as possible into each day. But he appreciated this ability of mine, which I'd like to try to pass on to you now. Here's how you can do what needs to be done each day.

First, energize yourself. Without energy, you cannot accomplish anything. Of course, you already know that a good night's sleep is of vital importance. But there is another re-energizing method available to you: I've found spending at least ten minutes each morning in prayer and meditation is quite helpful. During these ten-minute periods, you are waiting on God, getting closer and closer to Him. And God is the source of our renewed strength, mind and spirit.

Norman often quoted Isaiah 40:31: "They that wait upon the Lord shall renew their strength; they shall mount up with wings as eagles; they shall run and not be weary; they shall walk, and not faint." Then he loved to interpret the verse in his own words: "These words significantly teach a rare form of climax. One rises up like an eagle in a tremendous up-thrusting burst of energy. But the climax is to keep going when the going is tough, and not faint, which is another way of saying, 'Don't give up.' You get the energy for the long difficult trek, for the hard going times."

Norman also suggested that we personalize this biblical formula for energy by using this creative affirmation: "I am waiting on the Lord. Therefore I am renewing my strength. I am mounting up with wings like an eagle. I can run and not grow tired. I can walk when the walking is not easy. And I shall never have to stop going. I thank God for this miracle of undiminished energy."

The fact that energy is renewed simply through prayer and meditation has been made evident to me many times in my life and in the lives of many others throughout history. So before you begin your day's work, you might want to take ten minutes or more to energize yourself, to get "filled up" with God. Then if you find your energy waning later in the day, take another ten minutes to boost yourself up and pray.

I've also learned that a cluttered mind depletes energy and causes disorganization. To avoid confused thinking that leads to a non-productive day, I make notes of things as they pass through my mind. For instance, if I want to mention an article idea to one of our editors at *Guideposts,* I'll jot down my thought and put it in a pile of such notes that I will later sift through. When I go through my notes, I put them in order of importance. We'll talk about setting priorities later. For now, let's go on to another important factor in making each day productive.

Second, get and stay enthusiastic! The president of a large company once told me, "If you have two people of fairly equal ability, but the less able person has enthusiasm, he will go further than the other person, because there is a self-releasing power about enthusiasm that tends to focus the entire force of the individual. Enthusiasm, like an infection, carries all before it."

I couldn't agree more. A person with enthusiasm always wants to learn, to accomplish and to do his or her best. Whether your work is housework or homework, corporate, factory or volunteer work, whatever it is, you'll find that your productivity rises as your enthusiasm rises. I've found that once I start working on a project, I can maintain my enthusiasm for it by looking for the interesting aspects of what I'm doing. Everything we do is of interest if we use our imaginations. For instance, let's say you work in an automobile factory and you perform the same tasks each day. Try looking past the job. Think about how this car you helped assemble will run for years, taking children to soccer games, carrying an elderly person to church, enabling a teenager to be driven off to college. We should see that the end results of all our work are positive. We must take the time and use our imaginations to look that far ahead.

You can plow right through your daily tasks, if you change the way you look at them. When you apply enthusiasm to a job, the job becomes alive with exciting new possibilities. To maintain this, you might do two things I've found helpful: First, repeat to yourself the following: "This job is really challenging. Thank you, God, for this opportunity to prove myself." Then every few hours, take five minutes to review the tasks you have completed. Once you look at what you've done, you'll feel encouraged and ready to cover more ground.

Third, don't procrastinate! There's a little bit of the procrastinator in all of us, whether we're putting off washing the dog or dealing with some pesky situation in the office. But inevitably we all have to deal with that which we put off. And the more tasks we put off, the more they pile up. This spells disaster, especially for someone easily overwhelmed by a heavy workload.

When I have a lot do, I get up at least one hour earlier than normal. This extra hour makes a big difference in what I accomplish. I go into my office at the Peale Center and I'm able to work with little interruption, since there are so few people around.

Another method I suggest for overcoming procrastination is keeping track of what needs to be done. I mentioned that I make notes throughout the day. I take these notes and put them into a list, which I then review. Priorities are moved to the top of the list. I consider a priority anything that helps another person. My next priority is to meet all of my own deadlines. And so on. Sometimes I find that I do have to put off tasks, because I need to give them more thought. But I always go back to those tasks after a day or two of praying about them.

The point is to determine right now that you are going to accomplish something you've been putting off. Then, plan the reward you'll give yourself for completing the job. I think tomorrow I'll finish writing that article I put aside days ago. Then I'll treat myself to that new book I've been wanting to read!

Finally, being more productive through the day means asking for help whenever you might need it. I learned a long, long time ago that I cannot do everything by myself. And I'm not hesitant about asking for help. (My secretary Sybil can assure you this is true!) This is a lesson we must all take seriously. Whether you're a homemaker or a boss or a computer technician, you need to be willing to admit it when you need a hand of help. If you take on more than you can handle, everything you do will suffer as a result.

Even the simple act of asking God for His help makes an incredible difference in allowing you to get things done. I remember a time in Norman's life when he didn't feel up to all the job pressures that were put on him.

He and I sat and talked about it one summer while on vacation. My advice to him was to tell the Lord that he couldn't handle all of those problems by himself. I also suggested that he ask God to take over his life, and believe that God loved him enough to guide him through these issues. Norman did just that. Instantly, an incredible change came over him. "Let's end our vacation and go back to New York at once," he said to me, "I want to get back to work!"

"Oh dear," I responded, "maybe I've gone too far with this." But once we did return, the job problems that haunted him were still there, but they weren't nearly as daunting, because Norman was different. He had turned to God for help.

I've discovered through the years that God wants us to work with all our hearts at whatever tasks He's given us to do. But thankfully, He's also given us people who are often glad to help out if we'll just ask, as long as we don't take advantage of them. Our job is to work hard at all we do. Some people might call this old fashioned, but really this is not backward looking, but rather forward looking. Staying committed to using our gifts so everyone can benefit keeps us moving ahead. And that's what our work is all about, isn't it?

⧫ TAKE IT WITH YOU! ⧫

"Take inventory of your gifts and priorities for work. How can you best develop them today so that others might benefit?"

9

The Gift of
Adversity

*I sought the Lord, and he heard me, and
delivered me from all my fears.*

—PSALM 34:4

⁂

*T*IS DIFFICULT FOR ME to forget one of the most frightening experiences of my life. Norman and I had just come home from a full Sunday of church and friends and shopping. We were still laughing and enjoying the day when we walked into our living room in New York City and found a message to call a surgeon at the University of North Carolina Hospital in Chapel Hill. My heart sank.

Our son, John, had been completing his studies for a doctorate at the university there. Norman picked up the phone to return the call, and I stood next to him, anxious and waiting. When Norman reached the surgeon, he held the phone between us so I could also hear what he was saying.

"Your son came into the hospital today in an emergency. He was in agony. So we've tested him throughout the afternoon and we've arrived at the diagnosis of inflamed gallbladder with probable pancreatic complications." I took a deep breath as he continued. "We're medicating him, trying to delay operating because it's too dangerous with a gallbladder in this condition. We hope to reduce the infection and bring down his temperature first and operate on him later."

"Well, Doctor," I whispered, "John is in your hands and he is in God's hands. You do what you think is best." When Norman thanked him and hung up the phone, we immediately went into prayer: praying for the doctor, praying for our only son and asking God to help us through this time.

By 11:15 that night, the doctor called back to tell us John had not responded to the medication. The situation was becoming very serious, and he did not like operating under such conditions. Again, he felt it was too dangerous for surgery. "But it might be more dangerous not to," he said. "I think I'm going to have to operate."

Then I heard myself repeat to him, "Doctor, he is in your hands and in God's hands. Dr. Peale and I will be with you in prayer. Bring him through this for us."

"I'll try mighty hard," he told us. Norman and I then faced each other and realized we ran the risk of losing our only son. We knew he was in great danger, but all our lives we had tried to practice the idea of letting go and letting God be in control of the situation. Still, it is never easy to let go of your own son when everything within you draws him to yourself. We prayed again and asked God for His help in achieving this.

The doctor had said he would call us back in about two to three hours when the operation would be over.

But he did not call us back. Four hours passed, then five. Six hours went by. We literally prayed all night long, and waited for the phone to ring. Even though no word had come from the surgeon, at about 3:30 in the morning, I had a strong conviction that it was somehow going to be all right with John and that I could leave him in the hands of God. I told this to Norman. He looked me in the eye and said, "Ruth, I had the same feeling a few moments ago."

By six o'clock that morning, the doctor finally called us. I picked up the phone and heard him say, "Mrs. Peale, I'm glad to report that John came through the operation successfully. He's very sick, but he's also a healthy young man. He's lived a clean life, and that counts when the chips are down. I think he's going to be all right."

It had been a long time since I had experienced such an overwhelming sense of the greatness and love of God as I did that morning. Later I learned that at about 3:00 A.M. the situation had become so serious that they brought the hospital's chief surgeon in to take part in John's operation. I also told the doctor I had been praying for my son all night. When he heard me say that, he told me, "I always try to work in partnership with God!"

Certainly, every family has its share of emergencies and difficult times. For us, John's surgery was a crisis that I have to admit frightened me a great deal. The thought of nearly losing our only son was a test I wouldn't wish on anyone. Though at first I was worried, all I could think to do was pray. And when we finally received the doctor's call, I suddenly had a renewed sense of God's faithfulness and mercy. In other words, what others might have called a great adversity, I now saw as a gift.

Throughout our lives all of us experience times of trial, challenge or conflict, and how we choose to confront them very often can make a world of difference. For instance, if I had given up on John and just worried all night long, I would have become bitter while probably making Norman miserable as well. But learning to give my concerns over to God helped me remember who's really in control. That is why I believe we can gain a great deal about living positively through the gift of adversities.

Please don't get me wrong, however; I am not suggesting we go looking for hard times or painful challenges. If we wait a little while, they'll come! No, I think we need to exercise wisdom in all we do. I don't know any person who has not had some level of trouble come their way, most of the time because of circumstances they had absolutely no part in. The bottom line is simply that life can and does hand us its share of hardships, yet how we choose to deal with them can make all the difference. I have come to believe that instead of running from difficulties or trying to pretend they aren't there, we need to see these as opportunities that we can learn from. When we do, we begin to re-shape our attitudes and get the most out of life.

Of course, conflicts, disappointments and trials come in all sizes and shapes at any time in our lives. For some people that might mean getting a cold that prevents them from enjoying an event they'd been looking forward to; for others, it might be failing in a career they'd tried for years; for still others, it could be the tragic loss of a loved one through an accident. Whatever the challenging experience, though, I know from personal experience that each can be something from which we grow in our faith and character.

Perhaps one place where conflicts can arise consistently is in a marriage. For instance, very few married couples escape the sometimes distressing challenge of in-laws. Norman and I had our share of it too. Though we were devoted to each other's parents, we both found them trying at times. For example, Norman felt that my mother was rigid and uncompromising, with little tolerance or understanding of people whose views or standards differed from her own. I had to admit that this was true. On the other hand, I felt that his mother, gifted though she was, could be domineering and possessive. And determined to have her own way. I noticed this especially when we were first married, and she always insisted we had to go to her home for Christmas. "I may not be here next year," she would say plaintively if I suggested going to my parents or making other plans. So we always wound up going there . . . and I always had to control and mask my resentment.

Both of us got along better with our fathers-in-law than we did with our mothers-in-law. This also seems to be the general rule; the sharp-edged jokes about in-laws are seldom directed at men! For whatever reason, fathers-in-law seldom seem to generate the kind of friction that mothers-in-law do.

Regardless, the way Norman and I decided to handle this potential tension was that from the start we agreed to discuss our feelings about the other's parents openly and honestly—and in private. We agreed not to get angry or defensive when the subject of in-laws came up, but to treat it as a kind of good-humored verbal pillow fight in which either of us could say anything within reason and not do any damage to the fabric of our own marriage.

And it was amazing how often the appraisal voiced was accurate but never admitted by either of us. There is always that fine line of fearing disloyalty. But such openness about these conflicts between Norman and me always brought us closer together and made for a depth of understanding that—believe it or not—was a great experience every time it happened.

"Your mother is so narrow-minded," Norman would complain. "Why does she have to object to my father's cigars? When she sees him light one, she acts as if she had found him breaking all the Ten Commandments at once. What business is it of hers? Why don't you tell her to cut it out?"

"What she really objects to," I'd reply with some disgust, "is that sometimes when your father's cigars don't taste right, he spits in the fireplace! Why don't you tell him to cut *that* out?"

Or I might say, "Why is your mother so full of fears and phobias about things? She's always sure that the worst is going to happen. She sees a disaster around every corner. I don't want this kind of timidity to rub off on my children the way it did on your brothers and you!"

"My mother's not timid!" Norman would counter. "She has a vivid imagination, that's all. At times she thinks you can be pretty callous. She told me that when she was with you in the park the other day, and John fell off his tricycle, you didn't even pick him up. You let some stranger passing by do it!"

"That's right," I'd say. "I knew he wasn't hurt. I wanted him to pick himself up. Your mother acted as if he had broken both arms and legs. That's just what I'm talking about!"

So we'd say to each other anything that came to mind, and I think it was the best possible form of ventilation. I also think that we each secretly wanted the other to defend his parents with fire and sword. After all, a person who doesn't love his parents isn't likely to have much capacity of love for a married partner, or anyone else for that matter.

Maybe our in-law exchanges sound a little silly today. And I have to admit that recalling the little things Norman and I used to get irritated by do seem to be funny and almost petty. Especially when I consider there are horrible conflicts occurring every day throughout the world: natural disasters, abject poverty, senseless violence, you name it, our marital conflicts seem trivial in comparison.

But our frank discussions had a point. In the midst of whatever adverse circumstance we encountered— whether it was in-laws or children or church matters— we always found it helpful to talk it through honestly and openly, without letting the situation get the best of us. That way, we were determined not to allow any adversity to distract us or overwhelm us. Communicating about it helped us keep a positive perspective. The difficulties then became opportunities for us to learn and grow.

Which is why I tell people now that when some tragedy (or near-tragedy) strikes, it is important for you to find someone you feel close to and talk it through. We have to be willing to express our concerns and feelings as they happen, knowing that this, too, is part of the healing process for us. And we have to be willing to listen to others whenever they are experiencing a variety of feelings as a result of a difficult situation.

With the recent terrible rise of violence in schools, I have noticed that more and more educators are relying on the counseling efforts of trained professionals to help these children and their families work through the trauma. They are brought to the schools to listen to the concerns of students who have witnessed some tragic event, and then try to help them work through their emotions so they can get on with their lives. In some cases, they continue to be available for an indefinite period of time, or they set up peer counseling programs so that young people will always know they have someone they can turn to. I consider this a valuable and essential service.

But more then that, it confirms to me the need to talk things out whenever the going gets tough.

Maybe that is also why we get so many letters at the Peale Center for Christian Living from people who have just lost their spouses to some awful disease, or who are experiencing the pain of having a friend betray them, or some other personal trouble. Perhaps they came across one of Norman's books and felt they could trust us with their problems. Yet I also think that the simple act of writing out their grief and sorrows in a letter has helped them communicate their problems and release some of their negative power those problems have over them. We need to talk about our troubles, and for some friends, writing letters can be the easiest way to do that.

Of course, some people can take tragedy and heartache and overcome both with determination and a loving spirit. My friend Naomi Wilden, who passed away in 1999, was one of those special people. When she was battling a devastating illness, she wrote us the following letter:

> *During the last year I have had three operations for cancer, the last one involving the amputation of my right arm and shoulder. I have been so thankful for God's presence during this time.*
>
> *I had quite a struggle deciding whether to let the doctors do the extensive surgery they felt was*

necessary. I read the chapter, "How to Use Faith in Healing" in The Power of Positive Thinking *several times and prayed for guidance. I came to the conclusion that the best thing to do was to let the doctors do all they could and trust God for the rest. Once I was able to put myself completely in His hands, I found peace and was able to go to the operating room without fear.*

I made a very rapid recovery and now, eight weeks after surgery, am making preparations to be fitted with an artificial arm. I have been amazed at the way I have been able to accept this handicap without bitterness and depression.

Naomi's attitude is a fine example of how we, too, could confront difficult circumstances. First, she honestly acknowledged her feelings and struggles. Then she sought help and wisdom, and finally she went to God over and over with her concerns. The result? The good Lord met her in the midst of an extremely tough time and gave her acceptance and courage. In turn, I believe He even used her attitude to help me and others see that, as the Psalmist says, we *can* seek the Lord and know that He will hear us and deliver us from our fears! We may not undergo trials as daunting as Naomi's, but whatever cross we're called on to bear, we can do nothing better than to put ourselves completely in His hands.

This is the philosophy we have built our work on both at Guideposts and the Peale Center for Christian Living. We have always believed that prayer is a crucial cornerstone for living and especially for encountering difficult challenges that come our way throughout our lives. We have experienced this power of prayer over and over.

About twenty years ago, our business offices were located in Carmel, New York. One morning, I got a call that a faulty air conditioner had started a blaze that severely damaged a wing of our headquarters building. Bad as it was, that fire helped me to see some wonderful things about our work, and oddly enough one of the things I gained was a new reassuring look at our Prayer Fellowship.

An immediate problem we faced was finding working space for people and equipment from the burned-out offices. So the room in which we held our weekly Prayer Fellowship was pressed into service. The piano got shoved into a corner. Tables and chairs where we'd sit and read prayer requests that had been mailed in were stacked up one on top of another. It looked as though our Prayer Fellowship would have to be postponed until we could find a suitable room. That's when I realized again how important that time of prayer communion was to all of us.

At 9:45 on the Monday morning after the fire, men and women appeared from the various departments as usual to pray, coming back like homing pigeons. It didn't matter to them that there was no place to sit in comfort; they sat where they could—on file cabinets, on desks, or mostly they stood. The important thing was to be together, to pray for those friends out there who were struggling with problems regarding family, money, health or any of the troubles that can often beset any of us—and our nation and world—in these difficult days.

Prayer Fellowship was—and still is—a vital tradition in our work both in Pawling and in our editorial offices in New York City. When *Guideposts* magazine was founded in 1945, we always started our week—as we still do—with prayer. We prayed for our work, for one another, and for whatever concerns we were facing. Gradually, however, as the magazine expanded and more and more people wrote to us, we included our friends the readers in those devotional times.

For over five decades now, we've met regularly to read the hundreds of letters that have come to us during the week, to ask God to watch carefully over all of those who are in special need. No one is required to attend the prayer time, and yet, they do. And today, we continue to receive hundreds of letters asking to be included in our prayers, so many, in fact, that our staff alone couldn't pray for all of them. We needed help. So we invited volunteers to join our Prayer Fellowship by receiving requests mailed to their homes.

Today, in addition to our faithful staff, we have over nine hundred prayer volunteers who answer *Guideposts'* toll-free prayer line and handle almost 254,000 requests a year. Twice a year, on Good Friday and again during Thanksgiving week for Guideposts' Family Day of Prayer, the Peale Center opens its doors. On those two days alone, five hundred volunteers pray for more than twenty thousand requests.

Why do we put so much emphasis on prayer? Prayer brings us face to face with the God who can move mountains. You only have to read the daily newspaper to see how great the need for prayer is out there and how it grows daily. Many of prayer requests are sent to us by children around the country who are readers of our children's magazines or who visit regularly the *Guideposts'* website. Their simple faith reminds me that in our troubled world today, there is such a need for healing that it can only be addressed on a sacred level. Prayer was always the answer to adversity, and in these difficult times, prayer is still our best help.

The late department store businessman, J.C. Penney, was a great friend of ours. Once Norman asked him the secret of his outstanding success in life. Without a moment's hesitation, he replied, "Adversity and Jesus Christ." We waited for his explanation, amazed at his quick answer. Then he continued, smiling, "Without both, I would never have amounted to anything!" Mr. Penney obviously believed that adversity developed his spiritual and mental muscles as a Christian as it sent him into prayer. And, of course, he knew Jesus Christ gives the strength to stand up to it and the wisdom to weave it into your life pattern to make you stronger.

Whenever Norman and I traveled around the country for his speaking engagements, I would meet people who often gave me new insights about prayer. One of the most unusual stories I heard came from a woman who was living in Atlanta in the early 1980s. She told me about working with God as her "space mover." I asked her to explain to me just what she meant.

Apparently, this woman had been deeply worried about a son who was living several thousand miles away from her. He had developed a serious drinking problem and his marriage had worn pretty thin because of it. He felt additional pressures from having three children under the age of five and from a demanding job that he felt locked into. To top it off, this young stressed-out father had an hour bus commute each way to work, and when he'd finally arrive back home in the evening, he'd be so discouraged that he often dropped into a bar near the bus stop before heading home to his family. He never seemed able to bypass that bar.

The woman told me that for several days she had worried and prayed, asking God how she could reach her son and help him with his problem. "If only I could be there with him," she thought to herself as mothers often do. "If only I could ride the bus with him and get him home safely to his family each night." Then she told me she had gotten an idea: "Why not ride the bus with him?"

So, the next morning at 10:00 A.M., when it was 7:00 A.M. in her son's time zone, she did get on the bus with him—in her prayers. She rode in the seat alongside him from the suburbs to the city, sometimes reminiscing about things that happened when he was a boy and sometimes silent—just loving him and praying that her son would ask for God's help in dealing with his alcohol problem.

That night, when he caught the bus for the ride home, she again boarded with him, riding beside him, loving him, praying that his early faith in God would be renewed. Twice a day, from then on, she'd remind herself, "Now's the time to ride with Dan," and then she'd commune with him and with God on the pressures Dan felt.

After a number of days of "commuting" with her distant son, she started to feel encouraged. Though it took a great deal of concentration, it also lifted her spirit to know there was a way, with God as the "space mover," to be closer to him. She kept up this commuting schedule with confidence that faith would work a change.

Some months later, visiting her son and his family at Christmas, she learned that Dan wasn't drinking anymore.

"You know, I have a long bus ride back and forth to work," he told his mother. "One day I got to thinking about my drinking and that bar. I'd thought of it other times, too, but somehow, day after day, morning and evening, the drinking kept coming up in my mind while I was riding that bus. Finally, I made the decision to stop, and once I did, even that bar on the way home didn't tempt me."

This Atlanta woman reminded me that prayer is a perfect vehicle—for communing *and* commuting. Prayer, indeed, can get you where you want to be. What's more, I have learned that it can move you from anxiety and worry into a place of peace and contentment whenever challenging times come. Learning to turn over our troubles and fears to God is the best way I know of dealing with the sometimes painful circumstances we find ourselves in. It is also one of the most basic principles of Christian living.

Norman and I once knew a man who worked as a clown. One time Norman asked him how he was doing and he replied, "Well, you know how it is. We all have our ups and downs, the bitter with the sweet." Norman hoped he wasn't worrying about anything in particular.

"Of course not," the clown said. "Why worry when you can pray?"

This struck Norman and me as a sound philosophy toward the natural human tendency to worry or to be afraid whenever trouble comes. If we say each day to ourselves, "Why worry when I can pray?" we would eventually get worry under control.

Praying dispels worry in two ways. First, it releases and activates your built-in strength—that often untapped strength God has already given you. You pray the strength out, you believe it to come forward, and you practice it into existence. Then the worry fades away. Perhaps you could memorize the verse I quoted at the beginning of this chapter from Psalm 34:13—it's an incredible statement, for it speaks of a miracle that can occur in your life through prayer.

The second thing prayer does is teach you to think—and that, too, eliminates worry. So many of us don't really think, especially with so many stimuli competing for our attention each day. Praying, though, activates the mind so that you can understand, and get increased knowledge and new perceptions. It helps you become more alert to faith matters, and more in tune with God's wisdom. All of this, in turn, gives you power over anxiety when difficulties come your way.

Certainly, we've all been up against situations which, because of their importance to us individually, needed all the power we could summon. But just because those times inevitably come doesn't mean we should ever say to ourselves, "I can't handle it." You *can* handle anything. With God, you are greater than you think. Why worry when you can pray?

To get yourself started on praying, write down your concerns or worries. One by one, pray to God about them, explaining the situation. Then surrender them to God. Tell Him that the outcome is in His hands, and that you'll accept His will in the matter. The more you do this, the less the burden of fear or worry will dominate your life.

Once we've learned the power of prayer, we would do well next to learn to relax. I have never met a worrier who wasn't also a victim of great internal tension. But when you pray, as I have already suggested, you become calm and confident. You have tranquility, so tension dies. When you're free from tension and your mind is clear, there isn't anything you can't handle.

Norman used to suggest that people sit relaxed in a

chair and think of their minds as the surface of a lake in a storm, tossed by waves and in tumult. But now the waves subside, and the surface of the lake is placid and unruffled. He'd tell them to concentrate, then, on a beautiful and peaceful scene you have beheld. Bring out the melody in each and slowly repeat a series of words that express quietness and peace. It might even be helpful to make a mental list of times in your life when you have been conscious of God's watchful care, and recall how, when you were worried, He brought things out all right and took care of you. Remember the words of the prophet Isaiah: "Thou wilt keep him in perfect peace whose mind is stayed on Thee."

I've found that several times during the day whenever I have a moment, I repeat that Scripture verse from Isaiah out loud if possible, so that by the end of the day I will have said it many times. Then I conceive of these words as active vital ingredients that permeate my mind, sending into every area of my thinking a healing balm. This is the best medicine I've ever known for taking tension out of my mind.

Even with prayer and relaxation, we still need to learn to take things as they come. In my preparations for dealing with both personal or professional commitments and challenges, I have always tried to develop several lists of things I needed to do. But no matter how many lists one has, no matter how well prepared someone can be, the uncontrollable still comes up. We need to learn to take things as they come and do our best in the moment.

What we have to remember is that there is no sense in worrying or despairing over past failures, present situations, or potential mishaps. As long as we truly do our best as praying, positive-thinking Christians, God *will* see us through.

I remember a man Norman and I both knew, a man who often felt defeated, discouraged and weak from the blows of life. One bleak rainy morning, he entered a diner for breakfast. Several others were there, but no one spoke to anyone else. Our miserable friend sat down and hunched over on a stool, trying to decide what to order for breakfast. Even that was a difficult chore.

Then at the other end of the diner, he noticed a young mother with her little girl. Suddenly, the child broke the sullen silence in the small restaurant by exclaiming to her mother, "Don't we say grace here, Mommy?" All eyes suddenly turned to her tiny face, and waited.

Behind the counter, the big, burly cook looked at the little girl and said, "Sure we do, honey. Will you say it for us?" Then he glared at the other people present and demanded, "Bow your heads, all of you!"

One by one, the heads went down. The little girl bowed her head, too, and, clasping her hands, said in a loud, precise voice, "God is great and God is good. And we thank Him for our food. By His hand we all are fed. Give us, Lord, our daily bread. Amen."

All of a sudden, the atmosphere changed. People began talking to one another, and the plain little diner magically began to sound like a home. All because a little girl wanted to pray and give thanks to God for her meal.

But more than the diner was transformed that morning. Our usually gloomy friend later told us how that experience was pivotal for him. He saw the little girl's faith and he, too, started to believe in God, to believe in other people and to believe in himself. And then he began to pray regularly, no matter how much rain was coming down outside. He experienced the power of prayer in the midst of adversity, and that made all the difference!

✎ TAKE IT WITH YOU! ✎

"Offer this prayer to God and begin to believe He will get you through your trials. 'Lord, may I have sufficient courage and faith in You to pass through adversity when it strikes my life. Amen.'"

10

*Still
Positive
after All
These Years!*

Finally...whatever is true, whatever is noble,
whatever is right, whatever is pure,
whatever is lovely, whatever is admirable—
if anything is excellent or praiseworthy—
think about such things.

—Philippians 4:8 (NIV)

A FEW YEARS AFTER NORMAN and I were married and had moved to New York City, I suggested we take a short vacation to England. It was the summer of 1934. Norman was close to exhaustion from having counseled many people and preached many sermons. That was also a difficult time in our country's history: The economic crisis of the Great Depression ushered in breadlines, unemployment and despair in proportions unmatched before or since. As always happens, the cultural pressures of society found their way into the local churches, so Marble Collegiate Church had its share of difficulties. Norman did his best to remind the people that no matter what, God was still in His heaven and man was still created in His image; therefore, there was no reason to feel defeated or to lose heart. Still, the spirit of discouragement that matched the mood of the city hung in the pews of our church. And my husband was tired.

He knew the message of hope and forgiveness he was trying to offer was sound and helpful. But it didn't seem to be getting across to the people. and they weren't responding to it as we had hoped. To Norman, with his sensitive spirit and inferiority complex, that could only mean one thing: there must be something wrong with *him*. I knew he needed to get away from all these sources of discouragement, and I was fortunate to be able to arrange a short tour of England's Lake District. We could leave our baby daughter, Margaret, with her grandmother for a short time, and visit the countryside of Wordsworth and Coleridge. I hoped the time away would help revitalize and refresh my husband.

It didn't work that way. Though the Lakes were lovely, and the cottages were quaint, Norman's mood of discouragement did not seem to lift. If anything, as the time grew near for us to go home, he became more troubled, and I got increasingly concerned. Usually, I could coax him out of his emotional despair. Not this time.

The crisis came in the little town of Keswick, in the Cumbrian hills. We'd been staying at a hotel with a beautiful garden shaded by elm and chestnut trees. Over afternoon tea and scones, Norman finally began to talk with me about his work.

He told me he had originally thought that coming to

New York was the right and selfless thing to do, though now he was sure we'd made the wrong choice. Yes, he had been successful in other churches, but New York City was too much for him. It was too often cold and impersonal, and the warmth my husband wanted to offer did not seem to be what it needed.

For two years he'd been preaching, he thought, with few, if any, results. Now he was facing his third year in a pulpit that evidently was too challenging for him. Did it make sense, he asked me, to try to go on with it? The church was not truly united behind him. Oh, most people had supported him loyally, but he knew others who did not. There were some who wanted more scholarly preaching, and others who would prefer a great theologian in the pulpit. Norman was no intellectual and never pretended to be one.

He sipped his tea and continued. Even in counseling, he said he felt his limitations were becoming more apparent all the time. His training at seminary had been too academic and theoretical for him to cope with some of the real and practical problems that he encountered with people on a daily basis. And if he couldn't cope with these problems, what was he doing there? Wasn't he being a hypocrite? Wouldn't it be better to step aside and let someone more qualified take his place?

"It's bad enough to be a failure," he told me, "but if you are one, it's better to face the fact, don't you think, Ruth? Face it and stop trying to pretend you're something that you're not?"

I glanced up at the trees and sat quietly, considering the depth of my husband's confessions. Then I recalled in my mind the sermons I'd heard Norman preach over the years, and remembered how much I personally had gained from the messages he delivered to his congregations. Finally, I turned to him, and said, "You want me to contradict you, don't you? You want me to tell you that you're not a failure. Well, I can't do that because right now, at this moment, that's what you are."

I had never spoken to him like this before and I wasn't sure what would happen. I paused a few minutes before I continued. Norman simply stared at the ground in front of him. I continued, "You're a failure, but not in the way you think. You're a failure because you've let yourself be overwhelmed by the fear of failure. You're thinking entirely of yourself, of your success and popularity—or lack of it. You're not thinking about what God may have in mind for you. Maybe He wants you to know despair so you can help despairing people. Maybe He even wants you to fail because it might be good for you. In any case, why don't you practice what you preach? Why don't you do what you're always telling other people to do: trust God, put your life in His hands, surrender yourself to Jesus Christ and ask for His guidance."

Norman shook his head. "I don't know if I can, Ruth," he whispered, "I don't know if I can get rid of myself. There have been times before when I thought I had. But now . . ."

"You can't do it by yourself," I said firmly. "But if you ask for help to rededicate yourself, you'll get it. It's strange that I should say these things to you, because they're your own words, Norman. I've heard you say them to countless people. Ask the Lord to help you get back to Him. You've lost contact for a little while, that's all. Once you're back in touch, these difficulties that seem so large will iron themselves out. The church will grow. You'll solve the counseling problem. It will all happen as soon as you let yourself become once more a channel for God's power and stop fretting about yourself."

Then Norman looked up at me and asked, "Do you really think so?"

"I know so," I said. "Go on. Right now, right here and now."

And with those words, Norman grabbed my hand, bowed his head, closed his eyes and began to pray.

That time of rededication was significant for us.

Later, Norman even called it one of the most profound and rewarding experiences of his life. Soon afterward, the gloom that had been oppressing him lifted. Before long, his sermons had more vitality, more insight, more assurance, and people began to urge their friends to come with them to Marble Collegiate Church. The empty pews began to fill up, and sure enough, people began responding to Norman's message. Soon, my husband even started writing down some of his thoughts about how to change your attitude and think on those things that are worthy and excellent, rather than on the negative aspects of life. Eventually, he put those same thoughts into a book, *The Power of Positive Thinking.* Perhaps you've heard of it?

Though that rededication was almost sixty years ago, I believe that if Norman and I were to have that same conversation today, I would say the same thing. God simply used me to remind Norman what he already knew: that asking for guidance from God is the best approach to positive living. And I'm convinced that it's never too late to make that kind of a rededication for living the right way. If the man many considered to be one of the world's great optimists, Dr. Norman Vincent Peale, could rededicate himself to the truths of God, we all can. Because if ever our country and world needed a new dose of positive thinking, it's now.

Since it was first published in 1952, *The Power of Positive Thinking* has remained one of the most published and translated books in publishing history. To be exact, it has been translated into forty-two languages and sold more than twenty million copies worldwide. But it is really just a simple book explaining how to live practically and effectively with God, a book whose time had come and whose idea is still relevant today. Norman liked to say that he only tried to write and present Jesus Christ and Christianity to the people of the time "as the most exciting, practical, and tremendous way of life available." Obviously, I think he succeeded, and I'm sure I'm not the only one who thinks so.

Because of the book's helpful, down-to-earth approach, it immediately received national media attention and almost instant popularity. Perhaps that was because people in the 1950s needed a new sense of hope and optimism. World War II had just ended and much of the country was recovering from those difficult days, in need of a fresh and encouraging vision for life. The same can certainly be said today. In these past few decades, people have encountered enormous personal pain through divorce, teen suicides, youth violence, or natural disasters; the nightly mayhem on television or in the movies doesn't help. No, it isn't difficult to see why people today are just as hungry for a renewed commitment to positive thinking as they were fifty years ago. I know I am, and I imagine you are too.

In fact, just a few months ago I read an article in the science section of the *New York Times* on positive psychology. It seems more and more doctors and therapists are seeing positive psychology—or positive thinking—as a way of helping their patients regain a perspective for healthy living. Strategies for this kind of "new" therapy try to get patients to focus their attention on the good things in their lives, rather than the bad. Some of the very phrases and concepts that Norman introduced in his book were even discussed in that article. So the timeless truths of positive thinking are just as essential for getting the most out of life today as they were in the 1950s, if not more so.

But no matter how much science or psychology helps us see the benefits of positive thinking, at its very foundation is a simple acceptance of God's will. My husband never wanted merely to reach a religious audience with his message of practical faith in Christ. He wanted all of the country to hear it as well, especially as they struggled with issues such as personal identity and morality. And just as the roots of most of the problems and unhappiness at the time when the book was first released came because people struggled to believe those traditional Christian values, so the same is true of our nation today. Norman liked to encourage people "to fill their mind with God." When our faith is strong, and our mind is full of God, it's mighty difficult for any negative thoughts to get into our lives!

As a result, people today still find power in positive thinking. As our children and grandchildren travel around the country in different capacities, they frequently bump into someone who tells them how much *The Power of Positive Thinking* (or one of Norman's other books) has meant to them. Certainly, it has left a legacy neither Norman nor I could have imagined on that vacation in England in 1934!

In 1993, just before Norman died, he received a letter from a man in New York City who was writing from the hospital room where his sister lay in a coma. She had been the victim of a horrible attack, one that had received national attention in the media. This man was deeply grieved by the senseless violence that had happened to his sister, and sat beside her around the clock, praying for her recovery. Someone handed him a copy of *The Power of Positive Thinking*, and the man read much of the book aloud as his sister lay in a coma. He wrote to Norman to thank him for how much his words had encouraged him during that difficult time. And when he finished reading the book, the man—miraculously—realized that he could no longer remain bitter toward his sister's attackers!

Yes, on a regular basis, we have the privilege of receiving hundreds of letters and correspondence from people in similar situations. Just a few years ago, for instance, my secretary handed me one letter that moved me deeply. It came from a woman who was a forty-one-year-old single mother with a teenaged son. She confessed that all her life she had been searching for something, reading new age books, attending seminars and consulting with a variety of the leading "gurus" of the 1990s. She learned to meditate, and listened to the tapes of many "enlightened thinkers" of the day. She wanted desperately to help lead her son on the right road, but this woman, it seemed, was never satisfied in her search for meaning, truth and significance.

Then she picked up a copy of *The Power of Positive Thinking*. Now she was writing to tell me how she discovered "that many years ago Dr. Peale had the 'formula' for turning our thoughts into reality, but unlike so many who came after him, Dr. Peale gave the credit where it was due. To God. God uses us as messengers to spread His love and Light." And after years of suffering from excruciating pain in her shoulder, this woman read the chapter in the book on how our bodies are created to heal themselves. At that point, she put down the book and asked God to send His healing light on her shoulder. She wrote to tell me that she had not experienced any pain in her shoulder since she prayed that prayer! I wrote her back to thank her, and told her all these experiences she described express what God will do for those who believe.

Belief in God is at the heart of positive thinking. How do we nurture that belief? Well, even though some people might find it irrelevant in modern times, I believe that the Bible—the book *The Power of Positive Thinking* was based on—is full of help for discerning how to come through life's challenges with positive Christian ideals. Whenever I am asked today what guidance I would give to the next generation, I often turn to those passages from the Bible that are certainly as important to me today as they were when I was a child in the early 1900s. From Scriptures such as the one from Philippians that begins this chapter, I have learned that the way you think is going to affect you all your life. Therefore, you have to be very sure of the thoughts you express to others. I also try to encourage young people to read everything they can get hold of that has a positive message—including the Bible—so they can begin looking for a positive perspective from which to approach their lives. I know that often their family will either impart positive or negative attitudes to them, but they need to begin seeing God as the link between their thinking and their lives. The main point I try to communicate is that if a person today thinks he can, he can!

Still, skeptics might ask what difference positive thinking will make in the lives of young people when so much seems to be competing for their allegiance. Without question, I believe it can give them the feeling they can do with their lives anything they want to do. With God as their ever-present help, they can develop an attitude of positive thinking that acts as a guideline and leads them into a satisfied, full life. That is no easy thing, especially since so many young people today have not been exposed to many Christian principles for living. Most have not picked up a Bible, let alone understand its language, values or stories. Consequently, they're asking the question, "There must be something more to life."

So this type of Christian faith has to be presented in new ways to this "un-churched" generation. Helping young people find their way to traditional Christian values rather than some negative belief system is perhaps the greatest gift we could give them. There are so many exciting possibilities with positive thinking, because your mind then becomes alert to opportunities to grow personally and benefit others. How do we develop such positive vision? There are simple steps we can take to create positive lives for our children, ourselves, and those around us.

Let's begin first by remembering that positive thinking is the belief in our own God-given self-worth and in the value of everyone else. That belief leads to self-confidence, respect for others, and a lifestyle that is based on strong Christian values.

It might be helpful also to define what a value is, that is, a principle that reflects an ideal moral standard by which individuals guide their own thoughts and actions . . . and from which society as a whole benefits. Of course, many people slip into the habit of negative thinking because they feel discouraged, depressed, lonely, isolated or stressed. They want results fast and easy.

But we all know life is not like that. Life is meant to be a challenge. When our minds are full of fear, doubt and clutter, good ideas can't get through. We get our best ideas and make our best decisions when we're relaxed, open to impressions and responsive to them. Even though I am ninety-four years old, I still make my best decisions the way I always have: after regular exercise, eating a lot of fruits and vegetables, and spending daily time in prayer. I know it sounds like a common-sense formula, but these simple acts really clear the clutter from my mind and help me focus on the things I believe God wants me to.

There are, of course, many other steps we can—and should—take to unleash the power of this positive thinking. Perhaps we can begin by talking about values with family and friends. Seven master values make up the core principles in our lives: honesty, courage, enthusiasm, service, faith, hope, and love. You can improve your life by identifying behaviors associated with each master value and by talking about them with family and friends.

Unless we clarify our values by talking about them, it's too easy to focus on the negative self-centered values of our materialistic culture. As a society, if we do not live by our positive values, we aren't likely to support one another.

Becoming value-centered counteracts the common tendency we have to be self-centered and negative. We can continue thinking everything is going wrong—or we can get into the habit of thinking we can be a part of the process that helps things turn out right. Temptation comes to all of us, but as Norman liked to say time and again, we have the spiritual weapons for gaining victory over it.

An insightful piece of wisdom regarding temptation can be found in the Apostle Paul's first letter to the Corinthians. We are told that no temptation will ever come to us that has not been faced by others. And if others can overcome it, so can you. God will give you a way out, if you turn to Him and develop a relationship with His Son. I know we can and must live in a sometimes corrupt world without allowing ourselves to become corrupt. And the more we stand up for our values, the more others will take notice and stand up with us.

Next, we can begin seeing *and* seizing the opportunities God puts before us. Many people see opportunity . . . but for some reason, they don't always seize it. Seizing opportunity takes a greater step of faith while requiring a plan, because opportunity often is more illusive than the tasks you face at the moment. You have to find a way to link the present situation with the opportunity that is before you. You can't just sit at a desk and think positively about something and then hope it will happen. Most of the time, you have to make it happen by taking the initiative—or at least helping make it happen. Keeping alive a plan—like keeping alive a marriage or a career or even hope—requires some sort of creative action.

So, if you have a positive, upbeat frame of mind, you will exercise your initiative, resourcefulness, creativity and judgment. You will develop a clear idea of what you can do, plan it and fill in more and more details every day. Positive thinking then will be reinforced when you begin to see results. Yet, to my amazement,

many people still ask me why they should think positively. They wonder what difference they can make
when things seem so beyond their control. This is dangerous thinking, I say, and then I urge them to set goals
and line up their course of action to go in the direction
of their goals.

When our children decided they were interested in
going to college, we spent many hours talking with
them about what particular schools would be best for
their interests. All three chose different universities as
a result, and set their plan of action to pursue their specific career goals, whether that led them down paths as
teachers, writers, or business leaders. Then when it
came time for their children to decide on college, they,
too, talked about and researched which institutions
would be most suitable to developing their gifts. I'm
glad they saw their opportunities and were courageous
enough to seize them!

But I have to confess: sometimes I am a little nervous
for what my grandchildren (and their children) will discover as they venture out into this troubling world. The
daily papers, television and radio focus mainly on the
negative events that come washing over us every day. I
try to encourage them instead to look for the good
news, to ignore the negative news. Positive thinking
encourages people to live by the values that have

endured and held societies together over time. Many people today are looking for those values again.

I tell my grandchildren that the best way to focus on the positive is to reach outside of yourself and help another person. You could drive an elderly person to the grocery store, visit a friend in the hospital or help a coworker finish a job that isn't your responsibility. Then you will feel the difference you are making in individual lives and the problems of the world get smaller. It's also important to remember that every day good people around the world are doing good things, but most of these things are not widely reported (except in magazines like *Guideposts*).

Once we've developed this positive perspective, well, we have to *stay* positive. No one likes a whiner, complainer or fault-finder. What people do like, though, are those types of individuals who display compassion, kindness and a can-do, anything-is-possible kind of attitude.

I loved the story that one of our magazines recently published by a woman named Patricia Baum, about her four-year-old son. When this little boy was told that a family he knew had lost their home and all of their pos-sessions in a fire, the boy began to put together a bas-ket of his precious plastic dinosaur collection, his favorite stuffed animals and his special blanket. He planned to give them all to the family in order to "keep the kids from getting scared at night." Somehow, this little child knew that for almost every negative thing that happens, there is a positive one. Our job is to look for it!

As you go forward in the adventure of learning to be a positive thinker, you will no doubt encounter many exciting opportunities. Each day can be a positive one, and that is a good place to start: one day at a time. But along this exciting road of positive thinking, you are also likely (as our family has) to meet some persons who will depreciate positive thinking as nonsense, or as a get-rich-quick scheme, or as a visionary procedure that is superficial and without much value.

If this happens, just remember Romans 12:14: "Bless those who persecute you: bless and do not curse." Turn a negative situation into an opportunity to love someone! Besides, just because someone tells you that positive thinking is no good does not make it so. That is merely his or her opinion, and since the critic has probably not studied or worked with positive thinking principles, that opinion is hardly authoritative.

I'll never forget when Norman once received a critical letter from a woman voicing her opinion that positive thinking had no value and condemning him in strong terms for foisting "stupid and worthless ideas on the public." Rather than get angry at her, Norman wondered if her lack of restraint and the personal criticism was because she was either emotionally upset or had experienced some failure of her faith in a crisis.

Do you know what he did? He telephoned the woman long distance and quietly thanked her for her letter! Then he expressed interest in helping her. She, of course, became much gentler, and confessed that her husband was an alcoholic. Apparently, she had tried to "send out positive thoughts" to her husband to cure him. But the same night she did, he came home in an especially bad condition, beat her and then smashed some of their furniture. In her grief and anger, she decided positive thinking was no good and resented Norman for writing a book on the subject!

Norman listened to the woman's story, and then talked with her about how best to deal with her husband. Finally, he persuaded this woman to hold on to a mental image of him as a well man, to put him in God's hands, and then to give God plenty of time. Norman then called the husband, developed a friendship with him over the phone, and encouraged him to join Alcoholics Anonymous. Soon, my husband was able to hear the reports that their lives and their marriage were slowly being rebuilt. The woman eventually thanked Norman for being "so nice and for not getting mad at me because I wrote that letter." Norman laughed. I have to admit, I was proud of the way he had helped another person see the benefits of positive thinking.

When I think back over all the incredible moments Norman and I shared in the past century, all the opportunities we have had to be a part of other people's lives, I am struck by God's goodness to us. Whether it was listening to Norman preach in the pulpit, on the radio, on the street, or at the dinner table, I always knew that he had been given by God some essential gifts and insights for his time. Granted, my husband did not always believe in himself. That happens to all of us. But I know that deep in his heart, Norman understood that to sustain a powerful, undeviating faith in God was the mark of a positive thinker. And so he always tried to help others find their significant place in life. More than anything, we wanted our work to lead others to know the secret of creative living: *believe in God, believe in life, believe in yourself and in your future.* For over half a century, we shared those fundamental truths with others and experienced together great joy as a result.

Yet as I near the end of this book and maybe even the end of a long and wonderful life, I am convinced that these "secrets" are just the beginning. Yes, life with Norman was always an adventure. Life was always exciting with him. I am thankful for such a full life of God's blessings with our family. Still, I know these things are only a taste of what is to come, that we will celebrate God's eternal greatness forever, that heaven will be a joyous home.

I wouldn't trade my life on earth for anything (and I'm still planning my one hundredth birthday party!). But I know the greatest part of it has been the gift of faith in a loving and good God through our savior Jesus Christ. We have always believed that the power of God within you is equal to any of life's difficulties. If you believe this, too, then a rewarding and adventurous life will be yours. That core conviction has sustained me all my life, and I hope it becomes your greatest joy as well!

❧ TAKE IT WITH YOU! ☙

"Today you have two choices: to be happy or to be unhappy. Ask God to help you choose to be happy and affirm the good. This is the beginning of the power of positive thinking!"

Index